OFFICIAL
FORTNITE
HOW TO DRAW

Ⓛ Ⓑ

CONTENTS

TOOLS AND MATERIALS

Before getting started, you need a few basic tools, including the right paper and pencils. Graphite pencils and thick, smooth plain paper are ideal for beginner artists.

Drawing Paper

There are a lot of options when it comes to choosing drawing paper. It varies in weight (thickness), tone (surface color), and texture. Start with smooth plain white paper so you can easily see and control your pencil strokes. Thicker paper allows for repeated erasing and working.

Pencils

Graphite pencils are labeled to indicate the hardness or softness of the mineral. Most pencil sets range from 9H (hardest) to 9B (softest). HB pencils fall in the middle.

Hard pencils are great for sketching light, thin lines that are difficult to blend or smudge. Soft pencils are best for shading and adding texture, producing heavy, dark strokes that seamlessly fill space on the page and blend easily. Most artists use a couple of different pencils when drawing to make the most of their different values, bringing their artwork to life quickly.

8B   3B   HB   H   4H   F

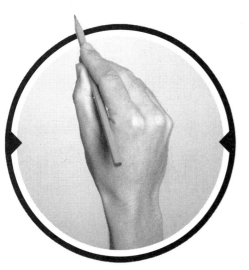

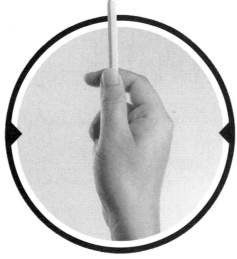

Holding a Pencil

There are two common ways to hold a pencil. Positioning your hand close to the end of the pencil gives you more control and precision but creates heavier strokes. This is known as the writing position and is great for detail work. Gripping the pencil further up gives you less control and precision but creates lighter strokes. This is known as the underhand position and is great for loose sketches, shading, and broad strokes.

Erasers

Erasers are versatile tools. Not only do they remove mistakes from the page, they are useful drawing devices themselves, able to add sharp highlights, emphasize light lines, subtly lighten areas of tone, and more.

Vinyl and plastic erasers tend to be white and have a plastic feel. They leave behind a clean surface and are gentle on the paper, making them ideal for removing any rough markings. Kneaded erasers are clay-like. You can mold them into any shape, making them perfect for adding detail to your work. Knead the eraser until it softens, then dab it over areas slowly to lighten the tone. Graphite sinks into the eraser. Simply knead it again to clean it.

Pencil Sharpener or Sandpaper Block

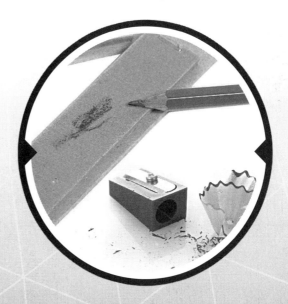

A sharp pencil gives you control over the quality of your lines. Handheld sharpeners expose the lead and create sharp tips, shaving pencil ends into cone shapes. To shape the pencil lead more specifically, use a sandpaper block. Hold the block in place, then rub the pencil tip over the surface to sharpen. Sandpaper blocks can also be used to clean dirty marks on your eraser.

BASIC PENCIL TECHNIQUES

Adding shading can make all the difference to your drawing. Just a few simple techniques can add depth to your creation, making it stand out on the page. Try to avoid shading in a stiff side-to-side direction, as this can create unwanted bands of tone. Instead, shade evenly in a back-and-forth motion over the same area, varying the spot where the pencil changes direction.

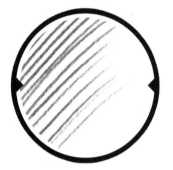

Hatching

This is a series of many parallel strokes going in one direction. Increase the value by applying more pressure or using a softer pencil. Angling your pencil makes thick strokes, minimizing gaps.

Gradating

To slowly transition from dark to light, apply heavy pressure to the side of your pencil and gradually lessen the pressure as you stroke.

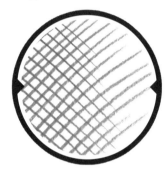

Crosshatching

This is a series of overlapping lines coming from multiple directions. Add another layer of hatching at an angle.

Shading Darkly

Applying heavy pressure to your pencil creates dark, linear areas of shading.

Shading with Texture

Use the side of the pencil tip to apply small, uneven strokes. This will create a mottled texture.

Blending

Smooth out transitions between strokes and create a dark, solid tone by gently rubbing the lines with a blending stick or tissue. Gradually add more graphite to build up darker areas.

TEXTURES

To show various textures in your drawing, you need to adjust your technique. Fur or cloth is shaded differently than metallics or skin. When shading, consider whether the texture is rough or smooth, and if it absorbs or reflects light. Use texture to build shadows and give realistic weight and form to an area. When using this book, you will draw a few different textures, including metal, cloth, and hair.

Metal

Metal is a hard, smooth, highly reflective surface, which means that any light will be very bright. This can create sharp, crisp edges and strong value contrasts. Polished metal is a mirrored surface and reflects a distorted image of whatever is around it.

Cloth

Cloth is a soft surface that absorbs light. This will create smoother transitions between highlights and shadows. Consider the material's density to determine the texture. For example, thinner materials will have more wrinkles that bunch together.

Hair

Hair patterns depend on the weight of the strands. Your pencil strokes will replicate the hair's direction and length. Long hair gathers into smaller forms. Simply treat each form as a sub-part of the overall shape. Long hair doesn't usually lie in neat, parallel lines. Curved areas will create a band of light.

SHADOWS

Light and shadows are key for bringing drawings to life. Artists use values (the different shades of gray between black and white) to define light and shadows while shading, which creates a 3D effect. Drawing lots of different values adds depth to your creation.

Identifying three elements will help you with your shading. The light source tells you what direction the dominant light is coming from, which will impact every aspect of your drawing. Areas that receive little or no light are shadows, and surface areas where light is blocked by a solid object is called a cast shadow. Identifying your light source will tell you where to draw the light values and shadows.

Once you understand your light source, you can add contrast. This will give your drawing a 3D look. Using extreme light and dark values rather than middle grays creates a powerful and dynamic high-contrast drawing. Using light and middle values creates a low-contrast drawing and is usually used for softer images.

HOW TO DRAW: WOOD

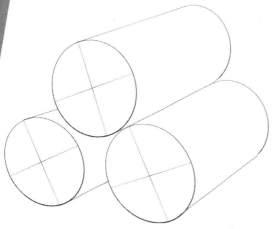

1.
Begin by lightly sketching three evenly sized cylinders, with one stacked on top of the others. These are your guidelines.

2.
Begin to add shape to the logs, drawing curves to create a more natural appearance. Sketch a few rings on the trunk.

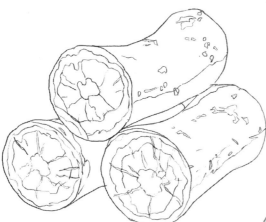

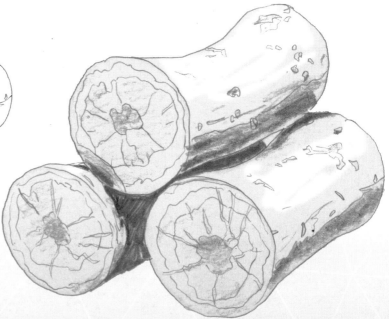

3.
Firmly pencil in your outline and erase any rough pencilwork. Give the Wood texture by adding cracks and chips to the logs, focusing on the center of the trunk.

4.
Finish by adding light value to your logs, paying attention to where shadows are cast in the woodpile and adding definition to the scars on the Wood.

HOW TO DRAW: METAL

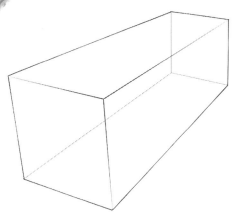

1. Metal is essential for building strong forts. To draw this material, start by simply sketching a long cuboid.

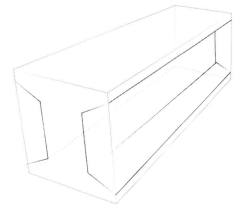

2. Begin to add shape to the Metal, creating a C-section cut-out effect along the side. This should make a capital I-section on the front face.

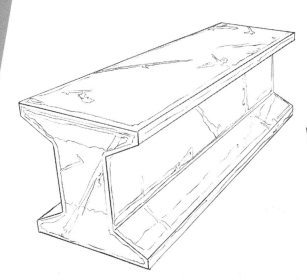

3. Firmly outline your final shape. Lightly pencil scratched details around the Metal and mark areas of shadows and reflection on the surface.

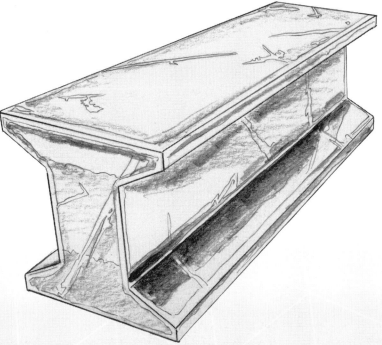

4. Using your guidelines, shade your drawing, working with four values: black, dark gray, light gray, and white. Begin with a light gray base tone and gradually build darker values.

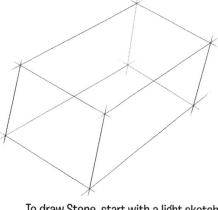

HOW TO DRAW:
STONE

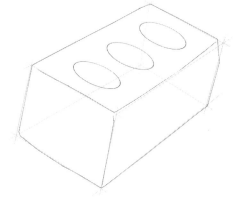

1. To draw Stone, start with a light sketch of a short cuboid, forming the resource's main shape.

2. Round off the corners and add cracks and three evenly spaced ovals for the core holes.

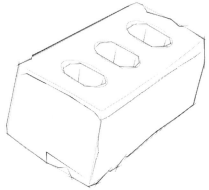

3. Add further definition, firmly penciling in the brick's overall outline, adding dents to the core holes and edges.

4. Add further chips to the Stone then lightly mark areas of value: black, white, dark gray, and light gray.

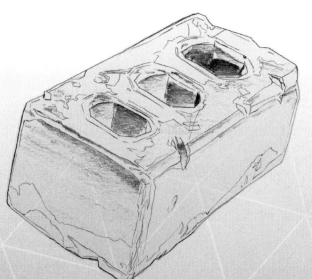

5.

Finish by using your guides to add value to the brick, using blacks and dark grays for shadowy areas, and laying a light gray base across the Stone's main body.

HOW TO DRAW:
HAND CANNON

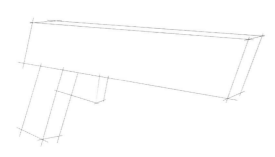

1. Start by lightly sketching the Hand Cannon's basic outline, made up of three connecting cuboids.

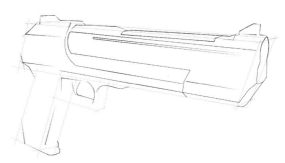

2. Round the corners then begin adding definition by lightly sketching the shape of the barrel, trigger, and handle.

3. Sketch details on the slide and muzzle before adding the safety clip and shaping the top of the handle.

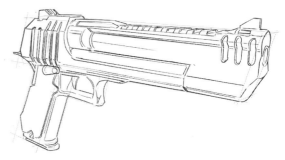

4. Once you're happy with the gun's shape, firmly pencil in the outline and details. Erase any rough guidelines.

5. Finish by adding high contrast value to your drawing. Follow the shape of the cannon with your strokes when shading to elongate the barrel.

HOW TO DRAW:
ASSAULT RIFLE

1. Begin by lightly sketching the loose outline of the Assault Rifle, building cylinders and cuboids together to create a rough outline.

2. Using your guidelines, sketch in the overall shape of the rifle's body. Round the edges around the stock and add a small wedge for the front sight.

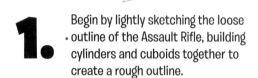

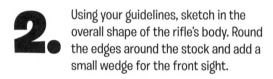

3. Add definition to the magazine and trigger box, as well as the ridges along the barrel.

4. Firmly pencil in the rifle's details, then erase any remaining guidelines. Add texture to the handle grip with crosshatching.

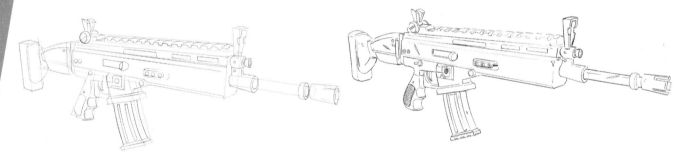

5. Finish by shading the darkest areas of the rifle with dark grays and blacks. Add light grays for shadows on the body of the gun, leaving the rest white.

HOW TO DRAW: BOOGIE BOMB

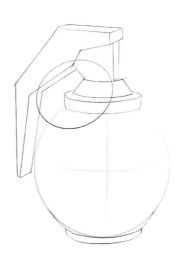

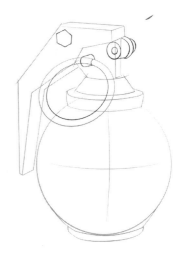

1. To draw a Boogie Bomb, simply start by sketching a circle, keeping the top quarter particularly light.

2. Draw the fuse, lever, and safety pin ring. Gradually build the shape, breaking the elements down into different shapes: cylinders, wedges, and a circle.

3. Add a small cylinder to create the lug and a hexagon for the safety clip before thickening the safety pin ring.

4.

Once you're happy with the overall shape, firmly pencil in the weapon's outline. Cover the body of the Boogie Bomb in squares to create a disco ball-like appearance.

5.

Finish by adding value to your Boogie Bomb. Have fun shading the body of the weapon, considering where the disco lights are shining.

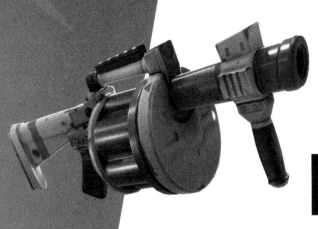

HOW TO DRAW: GRENADE LAUNCHER

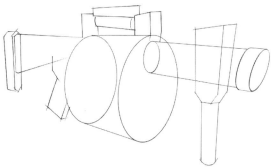

1. Begin drawing this explosive weapon by loosely sketching the base shape with a large cylinder at the center.

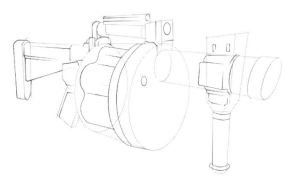

2. Add definition, focusing on the curved outline of the chambers, as well as the stock and handle.

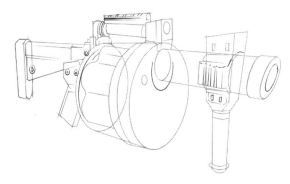

3. Pencil in the grooves and screws on the stock and handle, and lightly sketch the sight mount on top of the launcher.

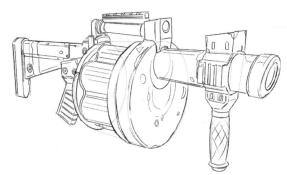

4. Firmly draw in the weapon's outline and add finer details, including dents on the drum and padding on the handle.

5. Erase any remaining guidelines before adding value to give the Grenade Launcher a metallic shine. To create the padded handle texture, use thick blacks in the center of each section, easing off the pressure toward the outer edges.

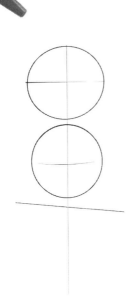

HOW TO DRAW:
CLINGER

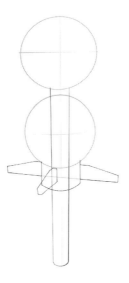

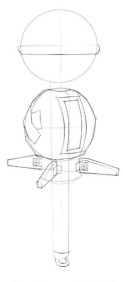

1. To begin, simply stack two equally sized circles, extending the vertical guideline down. Another circle should be able to fit in the space below.

2. Draw a long cylinder as the handle, using the vertical guideline as the center. Connect three wedges to a shorter, thicker cylinder.

3. Give the central circle a 3D appearance and roughen the edges. Thicken the horizontal guideline on the top circle. This will be the plunger's lip.

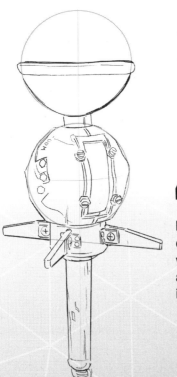

4. Firmly pencil in the overall outline of your weapon and add finer details, including screws.

5. Erase any remaining guidelines before adding value to your Clinger. Contrast thick blacks with bright whites to give the bomb a shiny metallic look.

15

HOW TO DRAW: ROCKET LAUNCHER

1. To begin drawing this explosive Rocket Launcher, simply draw a long cylinder topped with a cone.

2. Inside your initial guideline, stack three smaller cylinders, gradually increasing in size. Lightly sketch the handle and trigger grip.

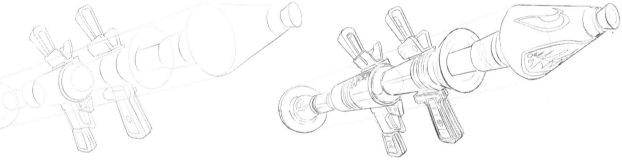

3. Sketch curves along the central cylinders. Add a small cone for the bullet's nose and draw the weapon's sights.

4. Define the weapon's outline before adding the finer details, including the fearsome face on the bullet.

5. Finally, shade your drawing using thick blacks and dark grays on the body of the gun, contrasting with the bright white of the bullet's head to make the features stand out.

HOW TO DRAW: COMPACT SMG

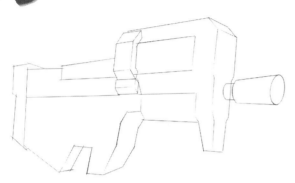

1. Loosely sketch the weapon's overall outline. Although the body is an unusual shape, it can be broken down into rectangles and wedges.

2. Using your guidelines, begin loosely adding the Compact SMG's features, keeping your pencils light.

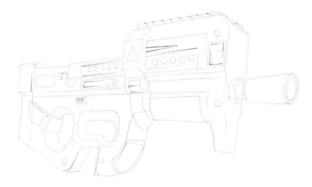

3. Pencil in finer details to give the grips and switches a 3D appearance. Round the edges around the trigger area and foregrip.

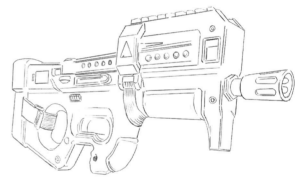

4. Add definition to the SMG by adding light lines to the fabric straps and holes on the muzzle brake. Erase any remaining guidelines.

5. Add value to your drawing, saving blacks and dark greys for the darkest areas of the weapon.

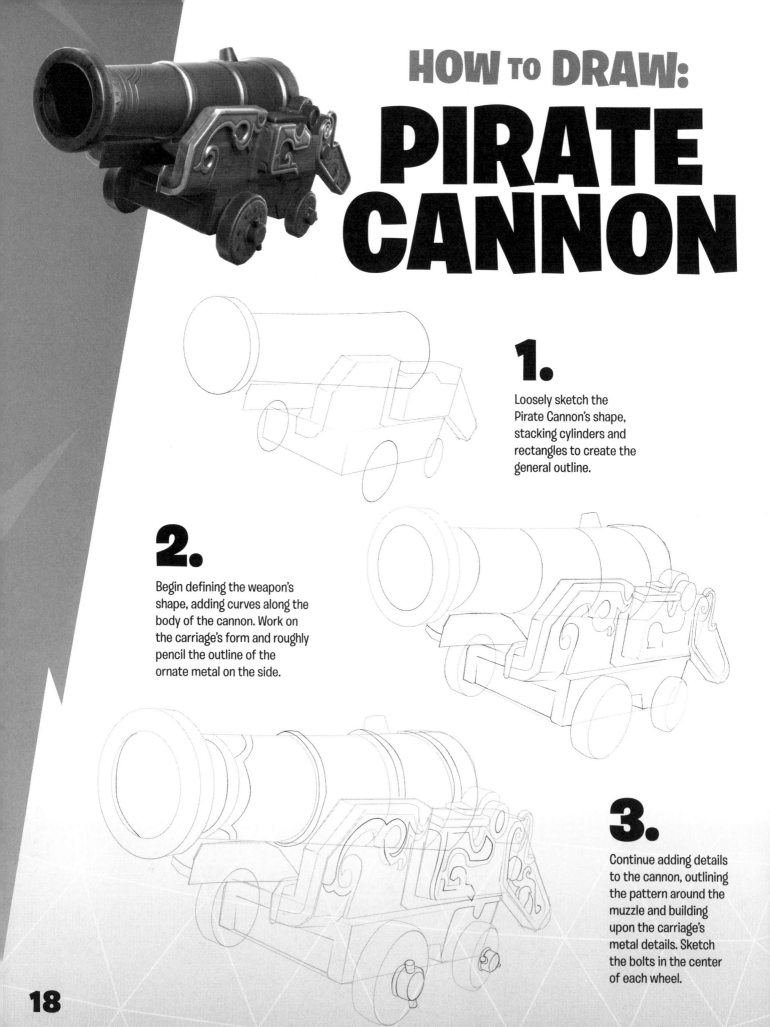

HOW TO DRAW: PIRATE CANNON

1.
Loosely sketch the Pirate Cannon's shape, stacking cylinders and rectangles to create the general outline.

2.
Begin defining the weapon's shape, adding curves along the body of the cannon. Work on the carriage's form and roughly pencil the outline of the ornate metal on the side.

3.
Continue adding details to the cannon, outlining the pattern around the muzzle and building upon the carriage's metal details. Sketch the bolts in the center of each wheel.

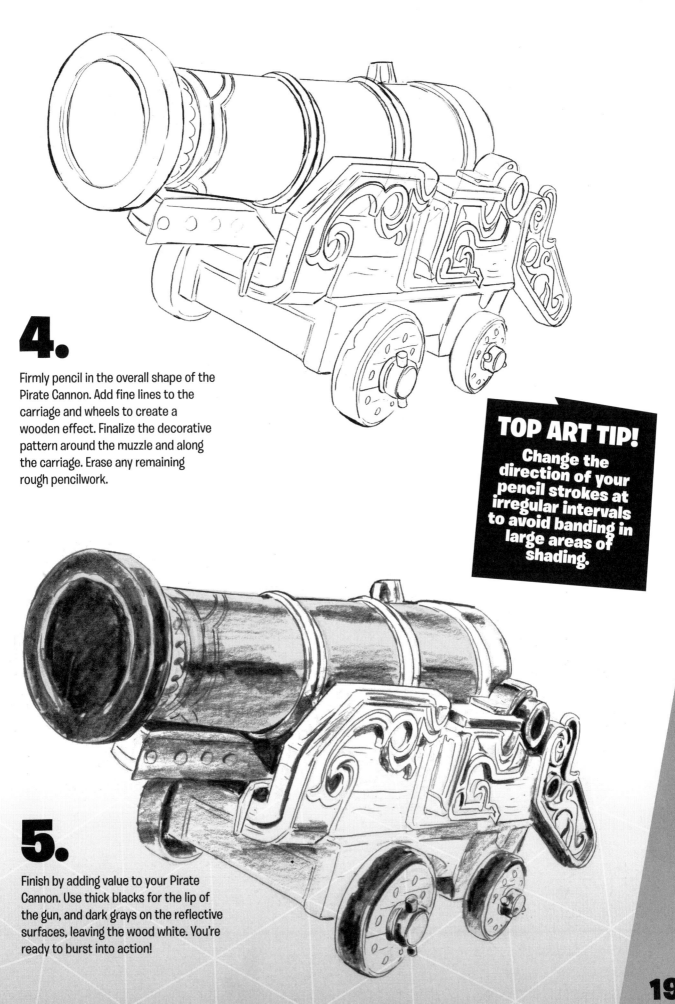

4.

Firmly pencil in the overall shape of the Pirate Cannon. Add fine lines to the carriage and wheels to create a wooden effect. Finalize the decorative pattern around the muzzle and along the carriage. Erase any remaining rough pencilwork.

TOP ART TIP!
Change the direction of your pencil strokes at irregular intervals to avoid banding in large areas of shading.

5.

Finish by adding value to your Pirate Cannon. Use thick blacks for the lip of the gun, and dark grays on the reflective surfaces, leaving the wood white. You're ready to burst into action!

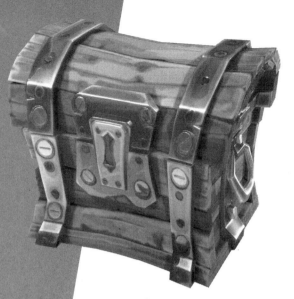

HOW TO DRAW: LOOT CHEST

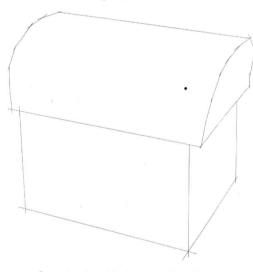

1. Start by sketching an initial outline of your Loot Chest, keeping the body big to hold weapons, ammo, and building materials.

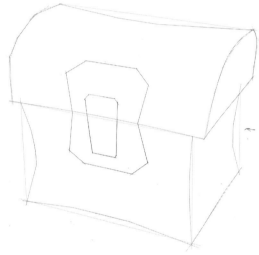

2. Begin adding shape to your chest, curving the lines at the front left and back right inwards. Loosely sketch the lock in the center.

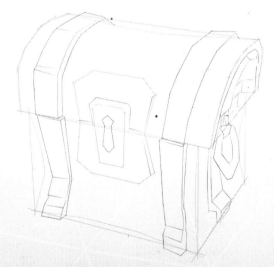

3. Begin adding 3D shape to the right face of the lid. Add the metal details, including the keyhole, handle, and straps.

4. Create a wooden effect by sketching rough lines along the body of the chest. Add screws to the metal areas, drawing different-sized circles.

5.

Begin creating texture on your Loot Chest. Consider where knots, chips, and scars might cause imperfections in the wood. Lightly outline the value changes.

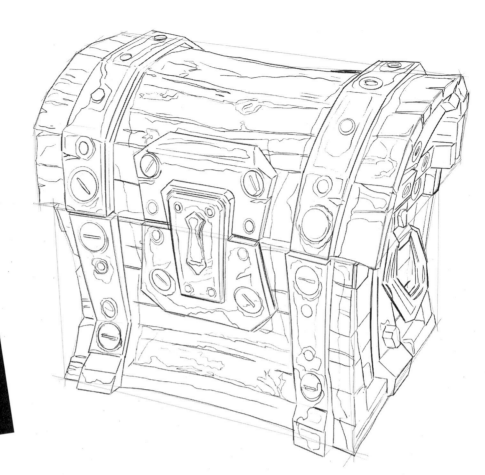

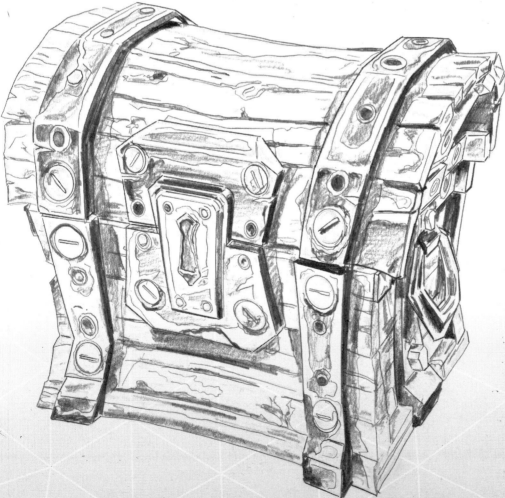

6.

Finish by adding value to your Loot Chest, focusing on the shadows surrounding the metal features. Circling is better than shading in straight lines for creating a wood-like texture.

HOW TO DRAW:
JETPACK

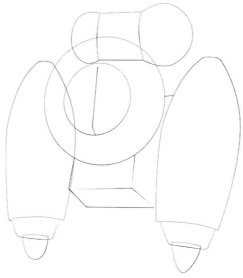

1.

Begin drawing this Legendary Jetpack by lightly sketching the overall shape. Although the item is symmetrical, we are looking at it from a slightly tilted angle. Perspective will make the features on the far side appear slightly smaller.

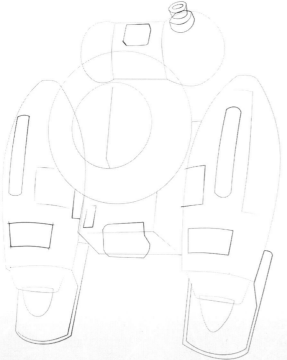

2.
Lightly sketch initial outlines for the Jetpack's details. Add the shields around each of the thrusters.

3.
Continue to build upon your framework, fleshing out your Jetpack. Add two curved tubes, attaching the fuel tank to the boosters.

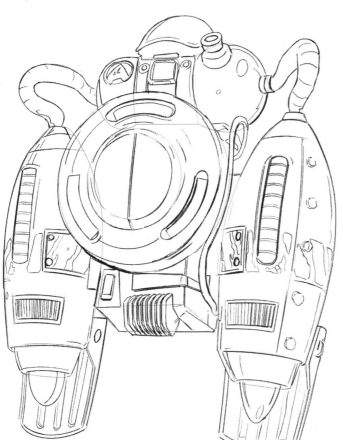

TOP ART TIP!
Use drawing tools to help create smooth lines and symmetrical shapes. A compass and ruler are essentials in an artist's tool kit.

4.

Keep refining the details on your Jetpack, adding bolts, reflective stripes, and the fire hazard symbol to the fuel tank. Lightly add curves to the tubing to create texture. Finalize the shape by firmly penciling in the outline.

TOP ART TIP!
Pay attention to the direction of your strokes when shading, following curves. This can add definition to your drawing, helping it fly off the page!

5.

Before taking flight, erase any remaining guidelines, then begin adding value. Shade with tight circles to create a more dynamic texture, revealing dents in the metal.

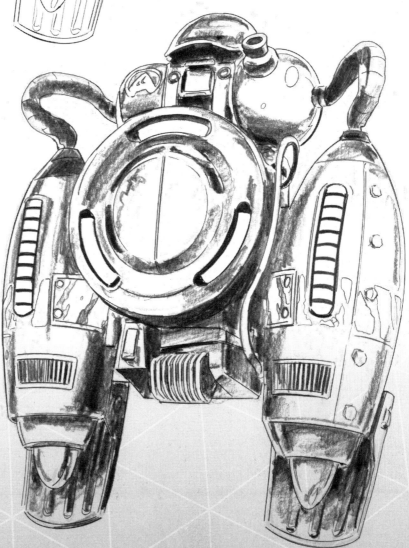

HOW TO DRAW: RAINBOW SMASH

1.
Begin by sketching the weapon's general framework, breaking each part of the unicorn head down into basic shapes.

2.
Add more depth to your Rainbow Smasher by transforming your starting lines into 3D shapes. Mark the eye placement.

3.
Begin to add detail to the face, drawing in the large eye, the reins, and an open mouth. Lightly mark hair sections on the mane.

TOP ART TIP!
Practice drawing 3D shapes to help you get used to drawing in perspective. Rainbow Smasher is made up of triangles, rectangles, and cones.

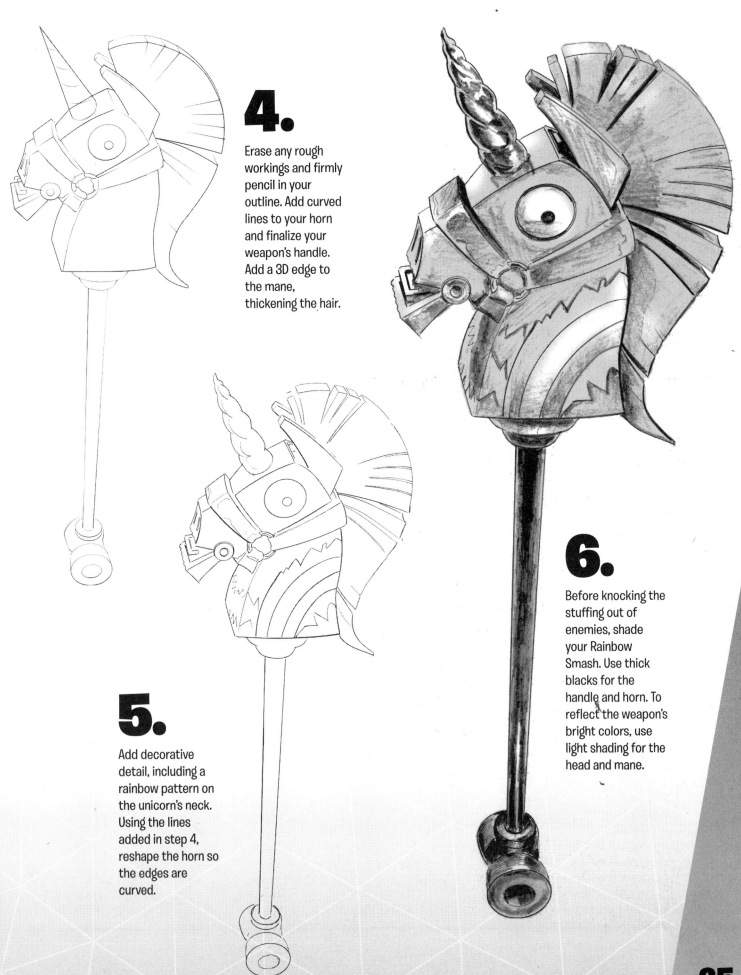

4.

Erase any rough workings and firmly pencil in your outline. Add curved lines to your horn and finalize your weapon's handle. Add a 3D edge to the mane, thickening the hair.

5.

Add decorative detail, including a rainbow pattern on the unicorn's neck. Using the lines added in step 4, reshape the horn so the edges are curved.

6.

Before knocking the stuffing out of enemies, shade your Rainbow Smash. Use thick blacks for the handle and horn. To reflect the weapon's bright colors, use light shading for the head and mane.

HOW TO DRAW: DEATH VALLEY

1.

Begin by drawing a rough outline for your weapon. For Death Valley, simply draw an oval and one long straight line for your handle.

2.

Thicken the handle. To the oval, add horn and eye placements and a small cuboid for the pickaxe head. The pick of the axe peeks out from behind the horns.

3.

Using your guidelines, thicken your pencil lines around the overall skull and weapon shape, the straps, horns, and eye. The skull's snout reaches almost halfway down the axe head. Add three small nails to the top of the skull.

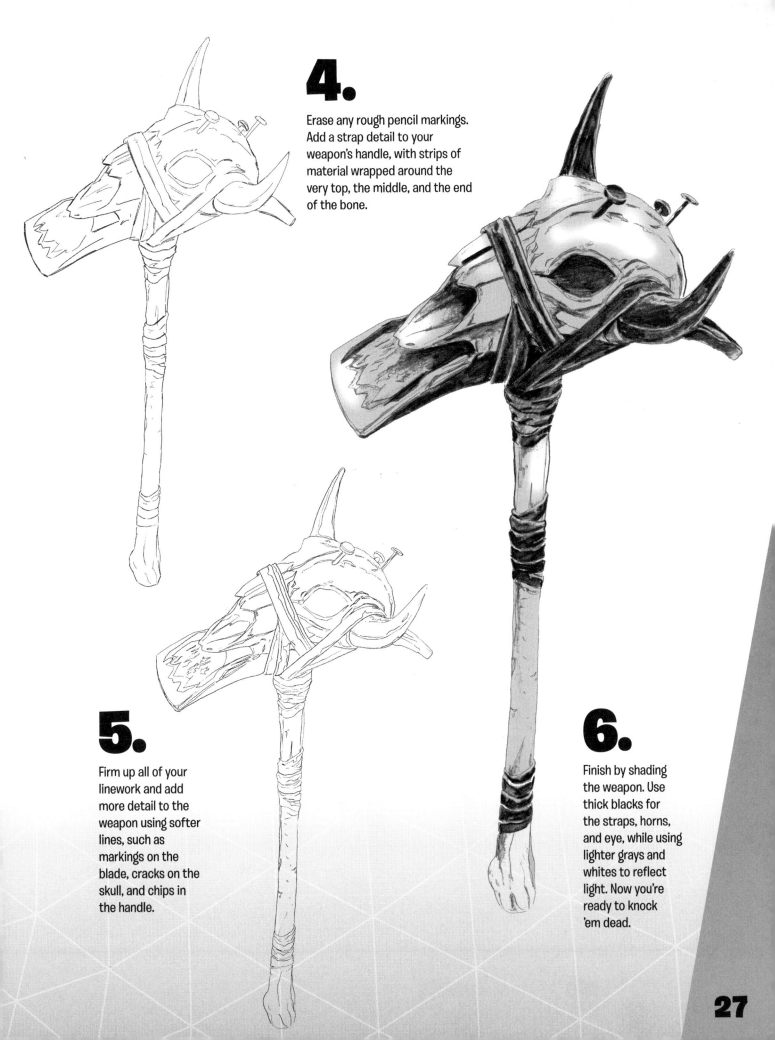

4.

Erase any rough pencil markings. Add a strap detail to your weapon's handle, with strips of material wrapped around the very top, the middle, and the end of the bone.

5.

Firm up all of your linework and add more detail to the weapon using softer lines, such as markings on the blade, cracks on the skull, and chips in the handle.

6.

Finish by shading the weapon. Use thick blacks for the straps, horns, and eye, while using lighter grays and whites to reflect light. Now you're ready to knock 'em dead.

27

HOW TO DRAW:
LLAMA

1.

Start by sketching a rough outline of your loot llama. Keep the body big so it can carry plenty of supplies.

2.

Begin to bring your llama to life by turning your line art into 3D shapes. Add a wide circle to the face for the large eye.

3.

Add the reigns to your llama's face, as well as the nose and mouth detail. Sketch a cuboid with a curved top on the side of your llama's body. This will be your loot crate.

TOP ART TIP!

Use your 3D guides from step 2 to help with rein placements around your llama's face. This will form the prism shape of the nose. Two thin rectangles form the nostrils.

4.

Draw in the hinges, upward arrow, and padlock on the crate. Thicken the legs then add some of the paper frill details to your llama, marking the area where the neck meets the body.

5.

Cover your llama's neck and body in the paper frills. Leave space for your saddle. Thicken your pencil lines and erase any remaining rough sketching.

TOP ART TIP!

The paper frills add texture to your llama. They will disguise your base outline. Placement can be random and doesn't have to be perfect, but try to ensure the body shape you started with remains the same. Make them different lengths to create a layered effect.

6.

Start adding shadows and shading to your llama, starting at the top and working your way down. Use a darker gray for dark shadowy areas and leave some frills white for contrast.

7.

Finish shading your drawing. Use thick blacks for the hooves and upward arrow. Leave the face white, except for some light shading around the eye to capture the llama's quirky look.

HOW TO DRAW:
WILD CARD

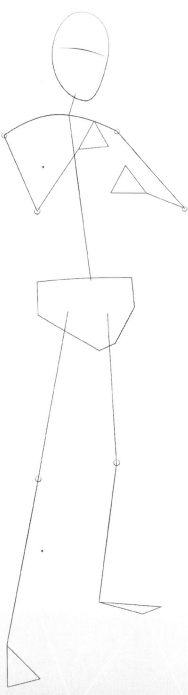

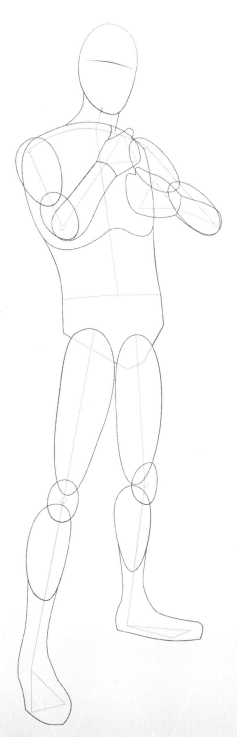

1. Stand out from the pack with this cool Outfit. Begin by drawing an initial framework of Wild Card with his arms in front of his chest.

2. Begin to add shape to your character. To reflect Wild Card's slim build, keep the outlines close to the framework.

3. Using your guidelines, firm up the overall outline of your figure. Begin to add definition to the hands and add eye placements.

4.

Sketch in the basic outlines of the costume's details, including the tie, buttons, and pockets. Add detail to his face, choosing your preferred card suit for his customizable mask.

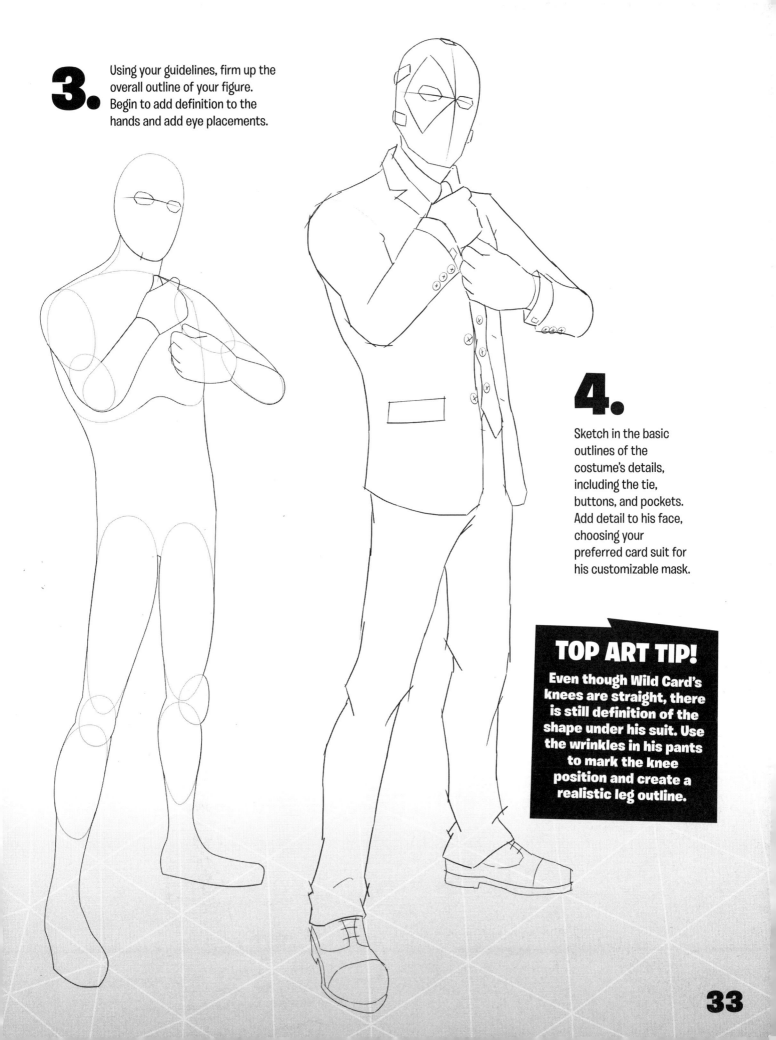

TOP ART TIP!

Even though Wild Card's knees are straight, there is still definition of the shape under his suit. Use the wrinkles in his pants to mark the knee position and create a realistic leg outline.

WILD CARD

5.

Use thick lines to firmly mark your character's final shape. Use lighter lines to pencil in the creases of his suit and the shine on his shoes.

TOP ART TIP!

Drawing Wild Card's hands adjusting his tie isn't too different from drawing a fist, just less tightly clenched. Keep the rounded shape of the top of the hand and sloping shape of the fingers in mind.

6.

Finish by adding value to the darkest areas of your Outfit. Use gradation to shade the shoes, using your eraser to highlight areas, creating an illusion of shine.

HOW TO DRAW: DRIFT

1.

Feel confident journeying into the unknown with this Legendary Outfit. Begin by drawing an initial framework of Drift with his arms out wide.

2.

Build upon your framework to add shape to your body. Notice Drift's palms are facing upwards and his head is tilted slightly to the side.

TOP ART TIP!

Remember to keep your pencil lines light when sketching your early stages. If you press too hard, they'll be difficult to erase later!

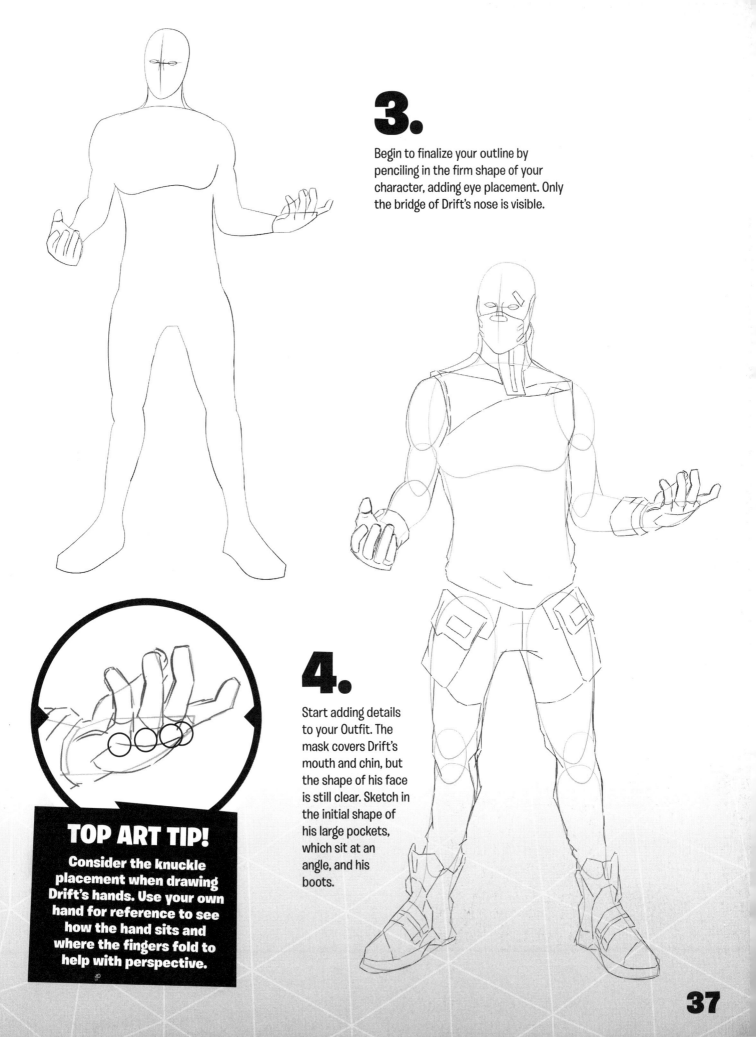

3.

Begin to finalize your outline by penciling in the firm shape of your character, adding eye placement. Only the bridge of Drift's nose is visible.

4.

Start adding details to your Outfit. The mask covers Drift's mouth and chin, but the shape of his face is still clear. Sketch in the initial shape of his large pockets, which sit at an angle, and his boots.

TOP ART TIP!

Consider the knuckle placement when drawing Drift's hands. Use your own hand for reference to see how the hand sits and where the fingers fold to help with perspective.

5.

Pencil in his facial features. Starting with the triangular shape at the top of his dynamic hair, draw curved lines down to meet the hairline in the middle of his forehead. Add a couple more spikes to create a 3D layered effect.

6.

Draw in clothing details, using lighter lines to add wrinkles to Drift's top and pants. Erase any remaining guidelines for a clean look.

TOP ART TIP!

The sole of a sneaker follows the same shape as the sole of a foot. Start by sketching a basic foot shape as a guide if you need extra help.

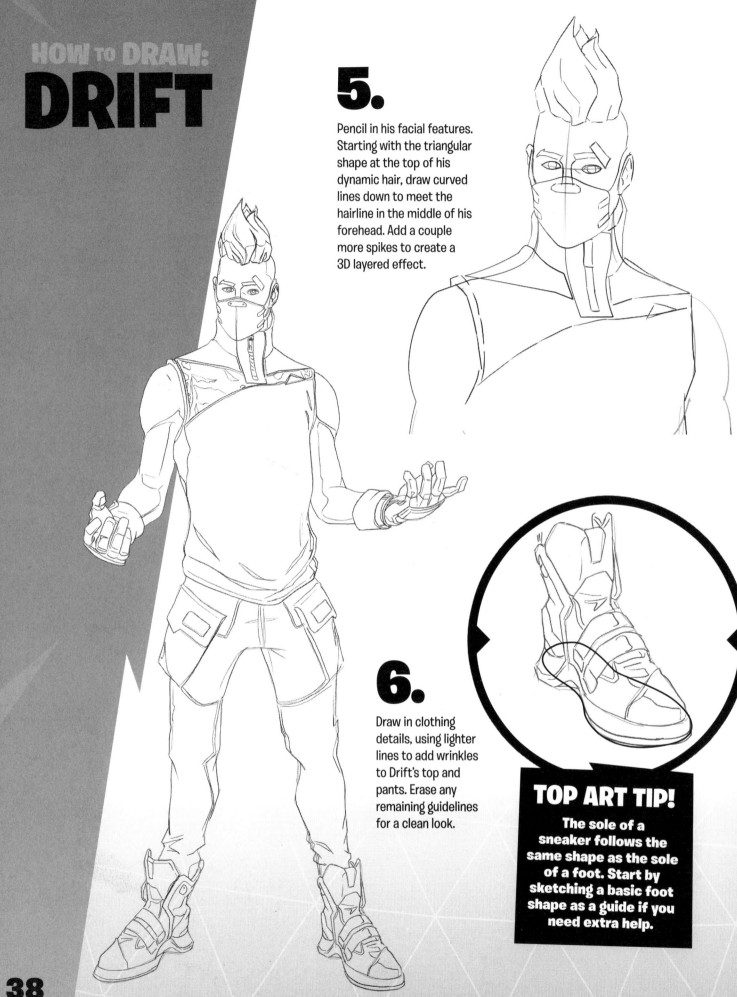

7.

It's time to shade your character. Drift's costume is mostly black and white. Use light and dark grays to reflect this. You're now ready to find your way to victory!

HOW TO DRAW: WHITEOUT

1.

Make your character stand out from the crowd with this futuristic Outfit. Begin by sketching the framework with Whiteout in a confident pose, hands on her hips.

2.

Draw in the base shape of your character's body. Notice the relaxed shoulders and heroic stance. Although Whiteout's suit largely conceals her feminine shape, her waist is pulled in slightly and her hips are slightly wider than a man's would be.

TOP ART TIP!

All fabrics will fit, hang, and wrinkle differently. Fitted clothes closely follow your body's outline, with simple wrinkles around knees and elbows.

3.

Using your guides, begin to finalize your outline by penciling in the firm shape of your character as well as placement for her Ignition Back Bling, slung diagonally across her back.

4.

Start adding detail to your Outfit, clearly marking the jacket, pants, and boots. Notice the hexagonal knee pads and thick shoulder padding. When drawing her helmet, use your face guides to ensure the visor sits centrally and at eye level.

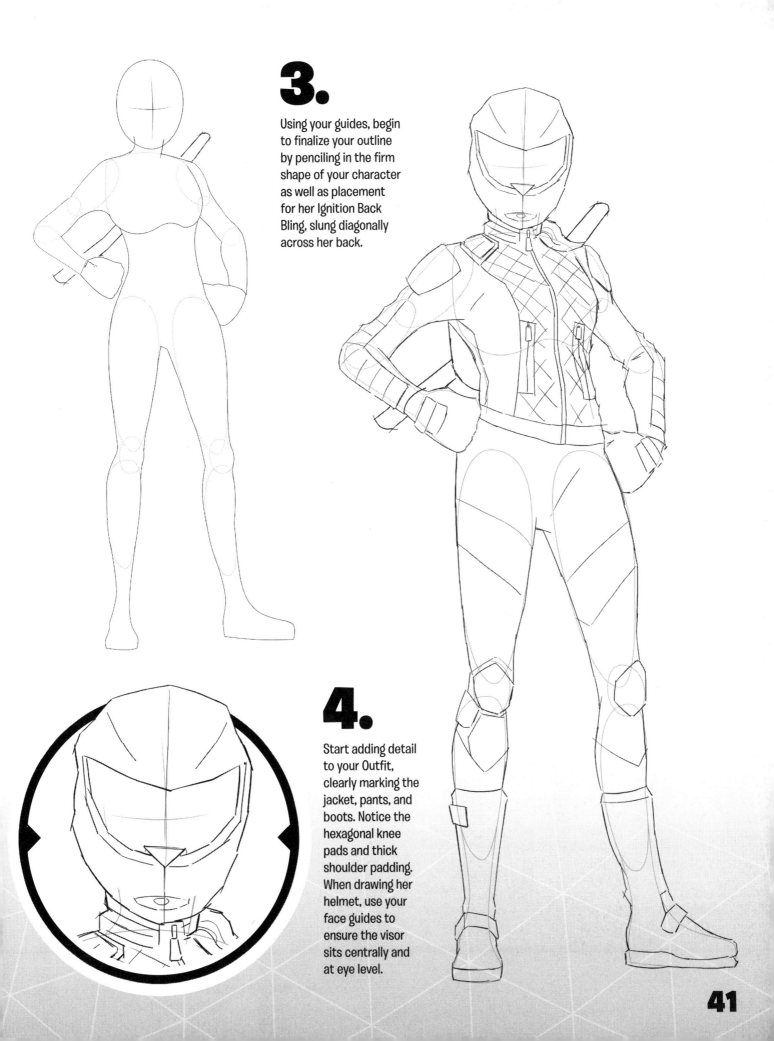

5.

Begin firming up your pencilwork, paying careful attention to the details on the clothing. Use lighter lines to add texture to the jacket. Erase any remaining rough lines.

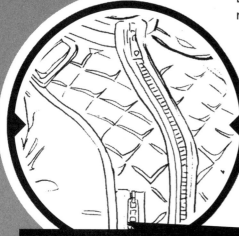

TOP ART TIP!

Whiteout's jacket detail is made up of lots of little V shapes, placed diagonally across her body. Draw a series of small rectangles for the zipper.

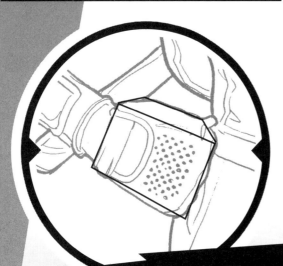

TOP ART TIP!

Picture Whiteout's fist as a large box shape with the knuckles curving at the point where her fist meets her hip. Mark each knuckle with a light curve.

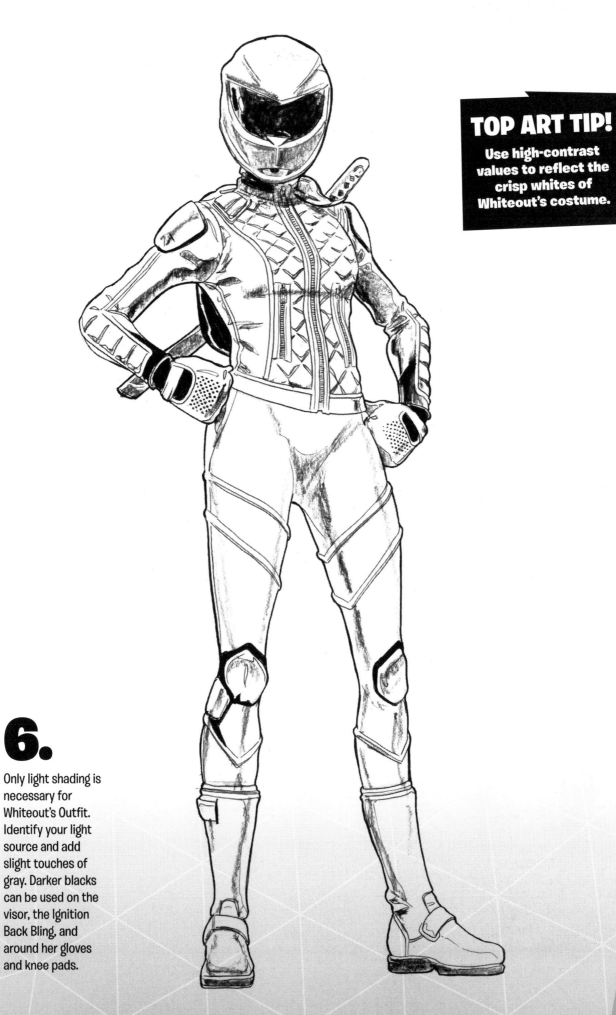

6.

Only light shading is necessary for Whiteout's Outfit. Identify your light source and add slight touches of gray. Darker blacks can be used on the visor, the Ignition Back Bling, and around her gloves and knee pads.

HOW TO DRAW: BUNNY BRAWLER

1. Hop into action by drawing this Easter event Outfit. Begin by loosely sketching Bunny Brawler's framework.

2. Build upon your initial sketch, adding shape to the body. Note Bunny Brawler's feminine figure is highlighted by her stance, with emphasis on the hips.

TOP ART TIP!

Use foreshortening to create the illusion that Bunny Brawler is leaning toward you. The proportions of your sketch will seem a little skewed, with some body parts looking larger than others.

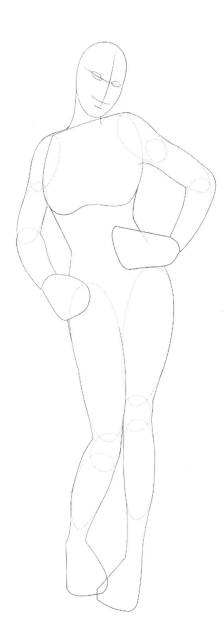

3.

Using your guides, begin to pencil in the final outline of your character's body. Sketch new guides for your facial features.

4.

Start adding details to your costume. Add curves to each side of the hood, topped with long bunny ears. Sketch in straps for her Eggshell Back Bling as well as the onesie's zipper.

TOP ART TIP!

Her adorable bunny slippers are the perfect example of foreshortening. Notice how the foot in front looks shorter than the one behind.

BUNNY BRAWLER

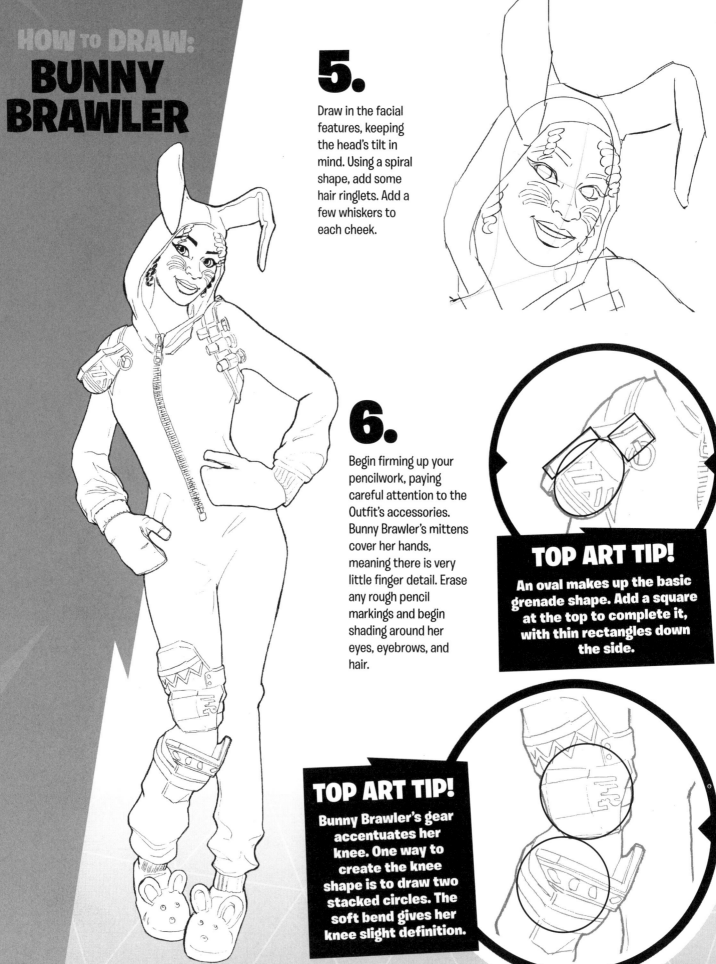

5.

Draw in the facial features, keeping the head's tilt in mind. Using a spiral shape, add some hair ringlets. Add a few whiskers to each cheek.

6.

Begin firming up your pencilwork, paying careful attention to the Outfit's accessories. Bunny Brawler's mittens cover her hands, meaning there is very little finger detail. Erase any rough pencil markings and begin shading around her eyes, eyebrows, and hair.

TOP ART TIP!

An oval makes up the basic grenade shape. Add a square at the top to complete it, with thin rectangles down the side.

TOP ART TIP!

Bunny Brawler's gear accentuates her knee. One way to create the knee shape is to draw two stacked circles. The soft bend gives her knee slight definition.

TOP ART TIP!

Catch enemies off-guard by reflecting Bunny Brawler's cute appearance. Use the side of a soft pencil to gently shade her costume.

7.

Finish by shading your character. Bunny Brawler's white onesie only requires some light shadow detail.

HOW TO DRAW: BEEF BOSS

1.

Start drawing this deliciously Epic Outfit by lightly sketching Beef Boss's framework.

2.

Add shape to the body by building upon your initial sketch. Beef Boss is not facing straight forward, so be sure to keep an eye on perspective.

TOP ART TIP!

Break the hand down into basic shapes when drawing a thumbs-up. Use a square for the palm and cylinders for the fingers and thumb.

3.

Using your guides, firmly pencil in your character's body outline. For Beef Boss's big burger-mask, draw a larger circle around your character's head.

4.

Begin adding details to your character's clothing. Add shape to the outer edges of the head to create the bun and filling. Draw in two large eyes and a long tongue. Don't forget the olive on top!

TOP ART TIP!
Loosely mark the belt to get the placement right, with the first one just above Beef Boss's hips. His accessories are made up of lots of rectangles.

BEEF BOSS

5.

Complete the details on Beef Boss's head by lightly adding sesame seeds and greasy marks on the tomato and cheese. Light lines will also add depth to his bow tie.

6.

Firm up your pencilwork and erase any remaining rough sketch marks. Add more light lines to his clothing to add texture. Draw in finer details, including the polka dots on his pants.

TOP ART TIP!

To create the lettering for the DURRR Burger logo, simply write each letter as normal then outline them to create bubble letters.

7.

Finish by adding value to your drawing. Minimal dark shadows are needed to create a high-contrast effect, reflecting Beef Boss's dynamic appearance.

HOW TO DRAW:
BULLSEYE

1.

Hit the target with this Rare Outfit. Begin by sketching a loose framework of Bullseye.

TOP ART TIP!

Understanding finger proportions will help you draw hands in any pose. The angles of your character's hand may change, but finger sizes remain the same.

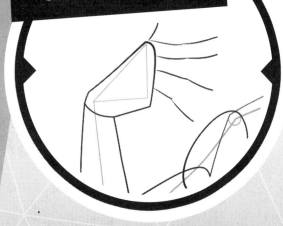

2.

Flesh out your initial figure, adding real shape to her striking pose. Note the angles of the body and her wide stance, with the viewer looking up at Bullseye.

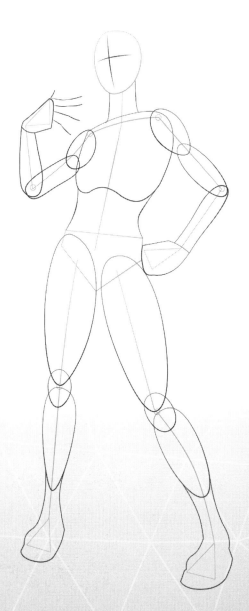

3.

Firmly pencil in the outline of your character's body and lightly mark on the facial features placement. Build upon your base sketch to create the fingers and glove shape of her left hand.

4.

Begin adding key details to her clothing, including a belt slung loosely around the hips and two knee-high boots. Draw her helmet and add the basic hair shape.

TOP ART TIP!

Bullseye's goggles are two thin cylinders. The distance between the lenses should be the same as the distance between her eyes.

5.

Start to add detail to Bullseye's face and erase any rough pencil lines. Add thin eyebrows and a half smile to capture her confidence. She is looking down rather than straight forward.

6.

Move onto Bullseye's clothing, adding the pattern to her camo trousers and the iconic bullseye logo in the center of her top. Erase any remaining rough lines and add light details to her arms, gloves, and boots.

TOP ART TIP!
The logo on Bullseye's T-shirt isn't a perfect circle. The shape of the target follows her curves.

TOP ART TIP!
When drawing boot laces, add the same number of loop holes on either side. Zigzag your way up the boot, missing a hole on each side as you go. Do the same on the other side, creating the crossover effect.

TOP ART TIP!
Bullseye's hair is separated into sections, each moving in a different direction. Use highlights on the curves and light shading to create texture.

7.

Finally, add value to your character, using thick blacks to define her eyes and high contrast to show off her bold personality.

HOW TO DRAW:
MERRY MARAUDER

1.

Begin sketching the framework of your character to draw this Epic Outfit. Notice his wide, open pose.

2.

Add shape to your figure by fleshing out your framework. There will be a bit of overlap on his thighs to create his wide stance. Don't forget his thick neck!

3.

Using your guides, lightly pencil in the overall shape of your character's body, clearly marking his clenched fists.

4.

Once you're happy with his outline, erase any guidelines. Sketch in the base shapes for his accessories. Using the face guides, draw in the shape of his mask, being careful not to fully cover his head.

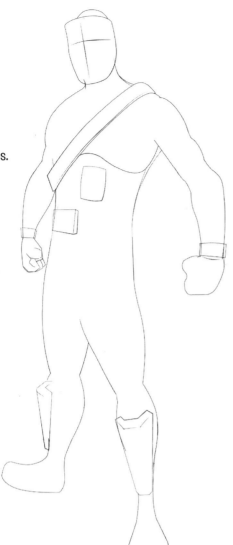

5.

Gradually add more detail to Merry Marauder's Outfit, including his bow tie, large buttons, and boots.

TOP ART TIP!

Characters with larger heads seem bulkier without appearing squat, which is where Merry Marauder's mask comes in! Draw it slightly wider than his face to add to the illusion.

6.

Draw the facial features on the mask. Two large circles sit at eye-width. Add a wide mouth, stretching across the bottom of the mask, and finish with some icing detail around the outside. This gingerbread man isn't so sweet, so make sure his eyebrows and mouth are turned down.

7.

Firm up your outlines and erase any visible guidelines. Have fun adding final decoration to your Merry Marauder costume, with lines of icing running across his knees, waist, and forearms.

TOP ART TIP!

The character's wide pose draws attention to his muscular arms. Notice that they're not simply round, but have various bumps and grooves to show off muscle definition.

8.

Finish by lightly adding value to Merry Marauder's entire Outfit. Lightly add shadows to his mask, clothing wrinkles, and inner leg. You're ready to slay!

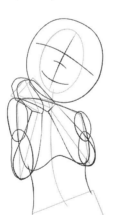

HOW TO DRAW: CUDDLE TEAM LEADER

1.

Begin drawing the cute but deadly Cuddle Team Leader by sketching a loose framework, both hands up by her chin and body tilted slightly.

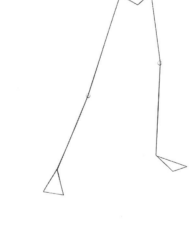

2.

Start adding shape to your character's body. Draw a large circle around the head and add guidelines for the mask's facial features.

3.

Begin to finalize your outline by firmly penciling the shape of your character. Mark on the outlines for the mask's eyes, nose, and mouth, as well as ears and a tuft of hair.

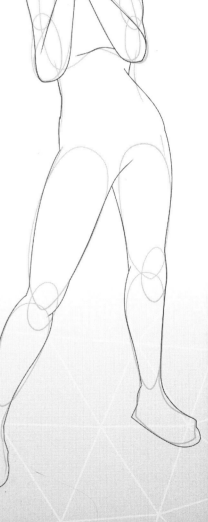

4.

Start adding accessories to your Outfit, including a belt and the Cuddle Bow Back Bling. Define the facial features by adding pupils to the eye and light fur texture. Turn the nose's triangle shape into a heart to add to her cute look.

5.

Firmly pencil in your character's outline and erase any remaining guidelines before adding more detail to the Outfit, including her broken heart logo and scar above her eye.

6.

Start shading your drawing. Begin by focusing on the darkest areas, such as the gloves, nose, Back Bling, logo, and straps. Leave some areas white to show where light hits the Outfit. Gradually add the fur texture to your Outfit, working from the top down.

TOP ART TIP!

Use a thick black to shade Cuddle Team Leader's boots and a very light gray for the laces. Use your kneaded eraser to create bright white contrast where the laces cross.

7.

Continue shading, laying down a light gray base tone over the Outfit, keeping it particularly soft on the eyes, ears, snout, and stomach detail.

TOP ART TIP!
Place a piece of blank paper under your hand when shading to avoid smudging your artwork.

8.

To finish, tighten up your shading, starting at the top and working your way down, adding shadows to the legs. Cuddle Team Leader is ready to hug it out.

HOW TO DRAW:
LEVIATHAN

1.

Start drawing your Legendary fishman Outfit by sketching a loose framework of your character. His head is more circular than other characters.

2.

Flesh out the shape of your character's body. Add a larger circle around the head. This will be Leviathan's fishbowl helmet.

3.

Begin to finalize your outline by penciling in the shape of your figure. Begin to add definition to his hands and mark eye placement. Notice how far apart they sit.

4. Erase any rough pencilwork on the body and begin sketching in the placement of the straps for his Fish Tank Back Bling.

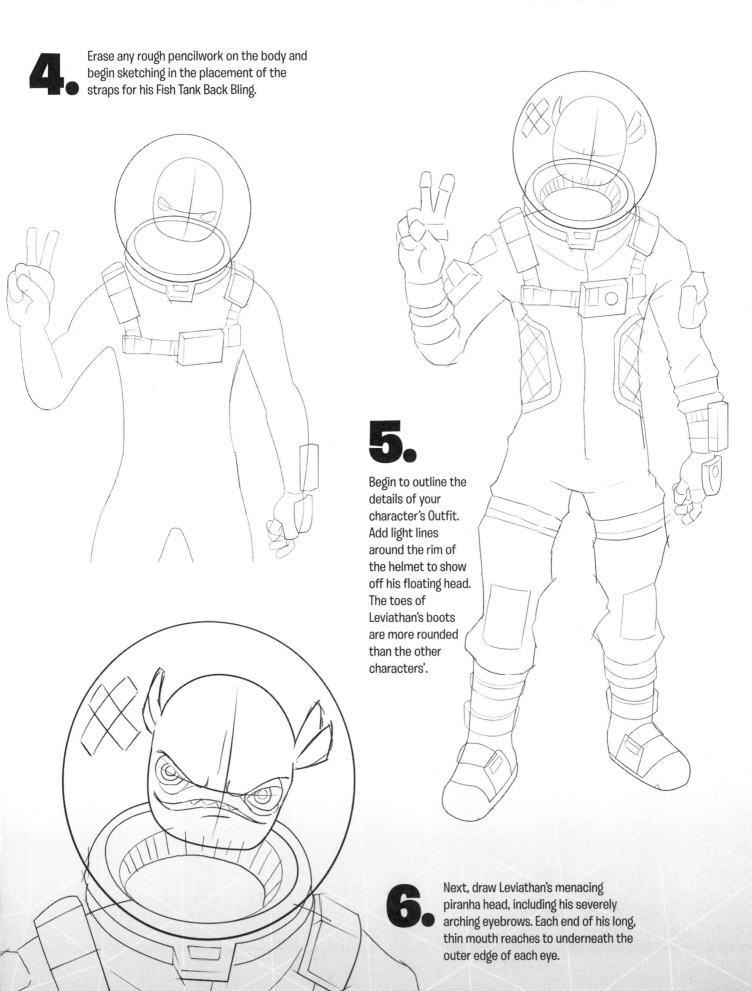

5. Begin to outline the details of your character's Outfit. Add light lines around the rim of the helmet to show off his floating head. The toes of Leviathan's boots are more rounded than the other characters'.

6. Next, draw Leviathan's menacing piranha head, including his severely arching eyebrows. Each end of his long, thin mouth reaches to underneath the outer edge of each eye.

TOP ART TIP!

Leviathan's hands are just like a human's, but with more definition around the knuckles. Add rounded cone shapes to the tips to enhance his otherworldly look.

7.

Begin to firm up your pencil lines, using thick blacks for your character's outline. Add finer details to the costume, focusing on crease marks in the clothing.

TOP ART TIP!

Leviathan's gadgets can be broken down into basic shapes: a cuboid on the back of his wrist and a shield on the back of his hand. Draw bold, crisp outlines to create a clean, futuristic look.

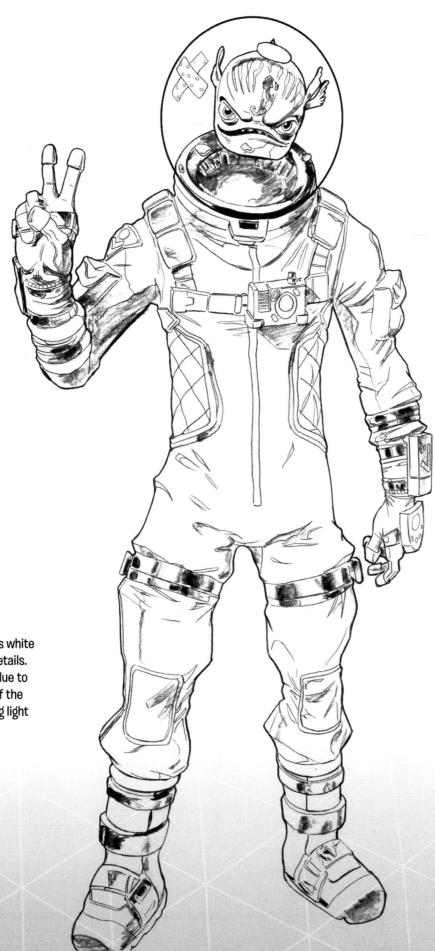

8.

When in full color, Leviathan's Outfit is white with gold ombre details. Finish by adding value to the golden areas of the clothing and adding light areas of shadows.

HOW TO DRAW:
CRACKSHOT

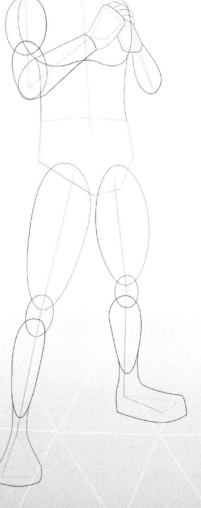

1.

Start drawing this Legendary Outfit by lightly sketching a framework of the body.

2.

Add shape to your sketch. Crackshot is an imposing figure, ready to fight. Note his clasped fists and larger head shape.

TOP ART TIP!

To draw bulkier characters, draw your body outline further away from your framework to show off their muscles.

3.

Firmly pencil in your character's outline. Widen the circle for the head to help guide hair placement before adding the base shape of the crown, marking the center.

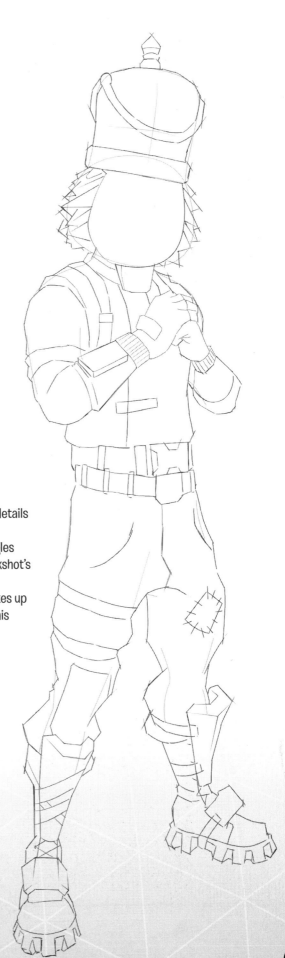

4.

Begin adding details to your Outfit. Layered triangles make up Crackshot's spiky hair. A trapezoid makes up the shape of his bottom jaw.

TOP ART TIP!

When making a fist, the middle sections of your fingers sit on an upwards angle. The palm curves to make a C shape which becomes gradually smaller as you curl your fingers.

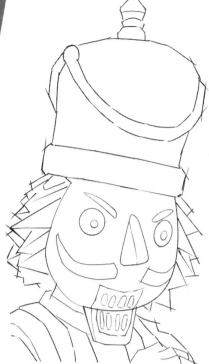

5.

It's time to add Crackshot's terrifying facial features. Use a large prism with rounded edges for his nose. His mouth is open wide, showing rectangular teeth, and don't forget his angry eyebrows.

TOP ART TIP!

To draw Crackshot's shoulder detail, draw a circle and an upside-down triangle, then join the two together to create a long tear shape.

6.

Add the finishing details to his uniform, using lighter lines on his clothing to give it a wrinkled texture. Light lines on his face help to make his expression look even angrier.

TOP ART TIP!

When drawing boots, start by drawing a circle in the sphere area, a wedge for the toes, and a cylinder for the leg to create your basic shape.

7.

Before heading out to crack some nuts, add some shading. Focus on where shadows fall and use dark blacks to reflect the darker colors of the Outfit. Work your way down from the top.

TOP ART TIP!

Cast shadows, such as the one Crackshot's arm has created, reveal the direction of the light source, which you can use to help with shadow placement on your own drawing.

HOW TO DRAW:
GIDDY-UP

1.

Start this wacky Epic Outfit by lightly sketching the framework of your character's body. His left arm isn't visible behind the llama, so stop at the shoulder joint.

TOP ART TIP!

Muscles move and bend with the bone. The L-shape of this character's arm tenses the bicep muscle, making it more rounded than an elongated arm.

2.

Flesh out your character, adding shape to his body. Although his torso will be covered, it is helpful to sketch it in here to ensure his body doesn't become too long.

3.

Begin to firmly outline your character's chest, arm, and legs. Lightly sketch facial features.

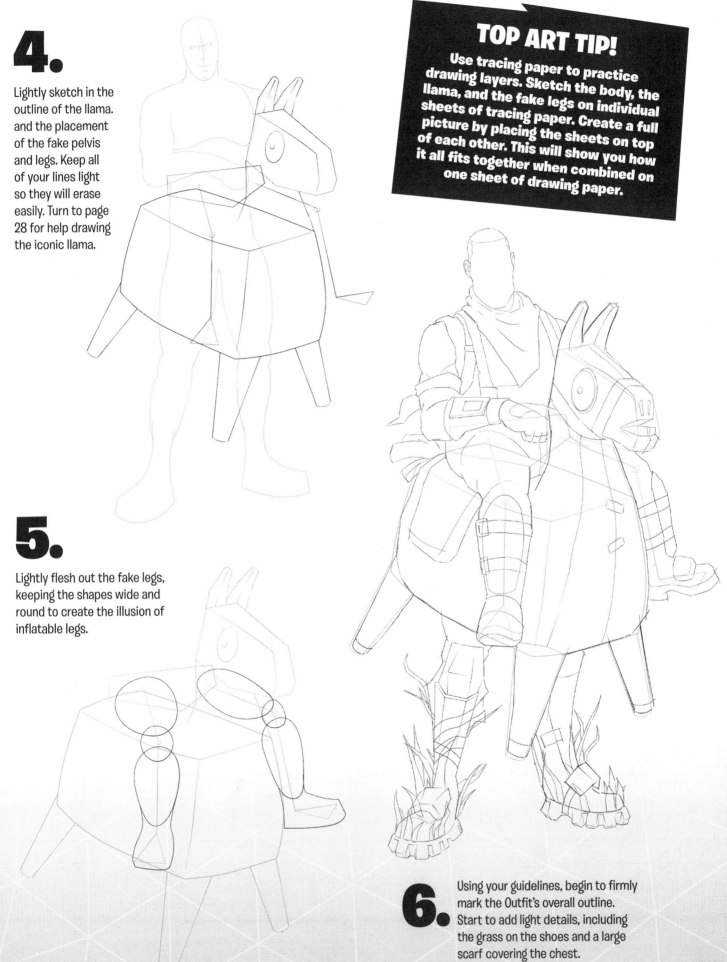

4.

Lightly sketch in the outline of the llama. and the placement of the fake pelvis and legs. Keep all of your lines light so they will erase easily. Turn to page 28 for help drawing the iconic llama.

Turn to page 28 for help drawing the iconic llama.

TOP ART TIP!

Use tracing paper to practice drawing layers. Sketch the body, the llama, and the fake legs on individual sheets of tracing paper. Create a full picture by placing the sheets on top of each other. This will show you how it all fits together when combined on one sheet of drawing paper.

5.

Lightly flesh out the fake legs, keeping the shapes wide and round to create the illusion of inflatable legs.

6.

Using your guidelines, begin to firmly mark the Outfit's overall outline. Start to add light details, including the grass on the shoes and a large scarf covering the chest.

7.

Draw your character's facial features. His face is quite long, and his cheekbones are defined. Lightly mark the outline of his hair. The Giddy-Up Outfit is fun, so be sure to reflect this by keeping his expression soft and happy.

TOP ART TIP!

While the blades of grass are simply long, thin triangles, have fun adding this detail by adding soft curves and bends in the grass to create varied shapes.

8.

Firm up your pencilwork and erase any visible guidelines. It's time to add finer details to your costume, including your character's tattoo. The llama isn't textured like the loot llama. Instead, add lines and rectangles to give him an inflated appearance.

9.

Finish by adding value to your drawing, working from the top to the bottom. Use thick blacks for the character's facial hair and hard grays for the shadows. Add minimal shadows to the llama's body to create the effect of the balloon reflecting light. Yee-haw! You're ready to ride into action.

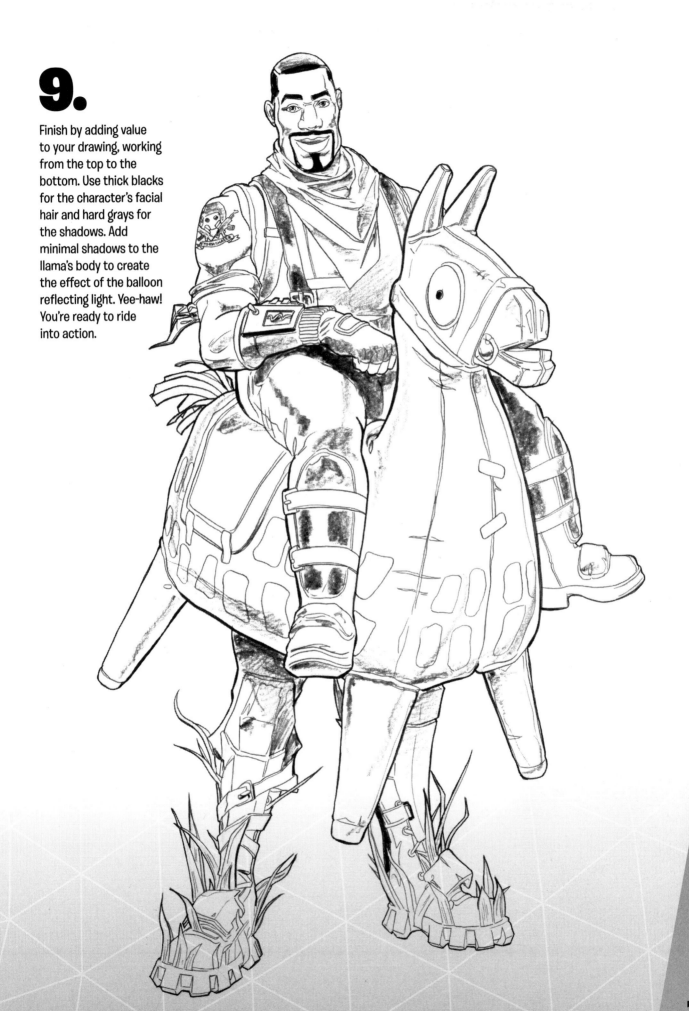

HOW TO DRAW:
DIRE

1.

Enter beast mode with this Legendary Outfit. Start by sketching the character's framework. Notice the second hinge in the leg below the knee.

2.

Begin to flesh out your character. The hunchback will make the head appear to hang low. Pull his waist in to contrast with the bulk of his upper body.

3.

Lightly pencil in your figure's overall outline. Add long fingers to his hand and rounded claws to his feet. Notice the sharp angles of his lower legs.

4. Draw Dire's facial features, with a mix of hard and soft angles. The ears are pointed and the eyes should be small under a furrowed brow. Draw a wide mouth with big, sharp teeth. Add triangle shapes to frame the face with large tufts of fur. Although it is an animal's face, human features should still be recognizable.

TOP ART TIP!

The guidelines for a wolfish face are slightly different to a human's. Curve the horizontal browline down, then bend the central vertical line at an angle where it meets the snout.

5. The outline of your character should be taking shape. Erase any rough guidelines, then sketch clothing and add initial patches of fur.

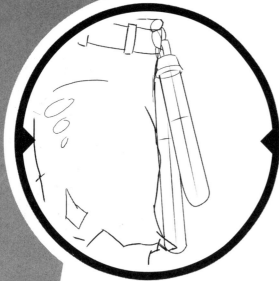

6.

Sketch in Dire's Wolfpack Back Bling. Stack cylinders to create the sword handle shape, with a thin square shape for the handguard. Add two cylinders to his hip for the nunchucks.

7.

Firm up your outlines and erase any visible guidelines. Use light pencil marks to add finer details to your Outfit, adding fur texture to Dire's upper body and feet.

8.

Finish by adding value to your character. Add dark shading around the eyes, nose, and claws, then use your kneaded eraser to create highlights. Add light shadows to his clothing.

TOP ART TIP!

Shade Dire's fur by drawing many overlapping circles to create a realistic furry texture. This technique is called circulism. The more circles you draw, the smoother the texture becomes.

HOW TO DRAW:
REX

1.

Channel your character's inner dinosaur with this cool Legendary Outfit. Begin by drawing an initial framework of Rex with his arms up, ready to hunt.

2.

Flesh out your sketched figure, adding real shape to the body. Notice the bend in his knees and his hunched shoulders.

3.

Using your guides, begin to finalize your outline by penciling in the firm shape of your character, creating the initial contours of the Outfit, as well as placement for eyes, nose, and mouth.

4.

Sketch out a square dinosaur face with pointy teeth and horns to make it look ferocious. Remember to leave the mouth open to show your character's snarling expression. Add a scarf and the Scaly Back Bling with more spikes curving down the back and a short tail at the bottom.

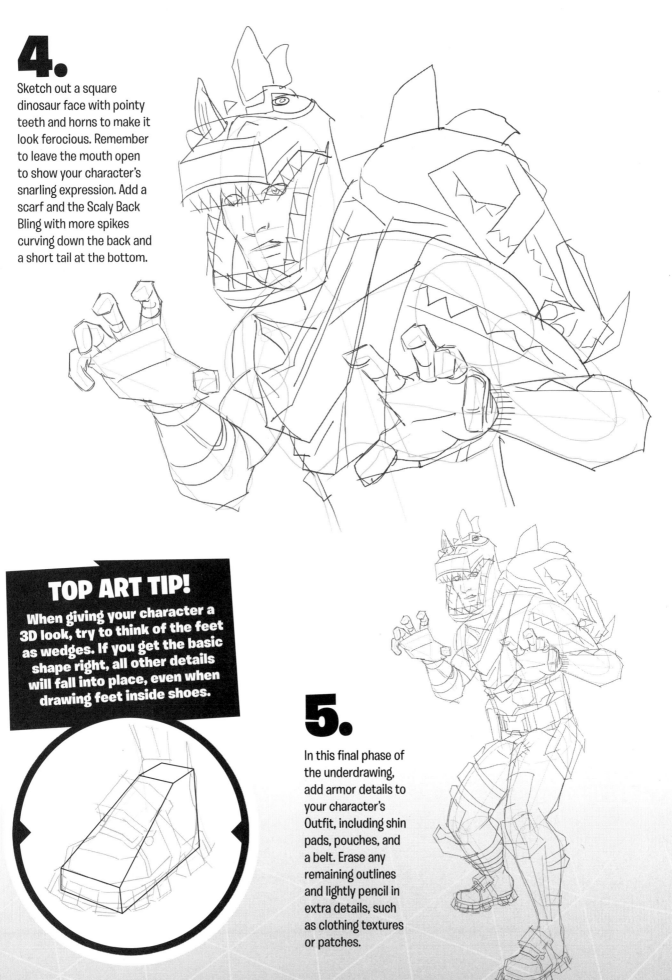

TOP ART TIP!

When giving your character a 3D look, try to think of the feet as wedges. If you get the basic shape right, all other details will fall into place, even when drawing feet inside shoes.

5.

In this final phase of the underdrawing, add armor details to your character's Outfit, including shin pads, pouches, and a belt. Erase any remaining outlines and lightly pencil in extra details, such as clothing textures or patches.

HOW TO DRAW: REX

6.

Firmly pencil in Rex's outline, taking care to add clear facial details to your character. Use lighter lines on details like textures to help bring your drawing to life.

TOP ART TIP!

Picturing each finger as a stack of three cylinders can really help with perspective when drawing hands. Start by drawing the cylinder stacks then blend into the finger shape, with the base of each cylinder acting as the joint fold.

7.

Begin the shading process. Remember to consider where shadows might fall on Rex, lightly shading or leaving white any areas which might be brighter.

8.

Finish shading your character. When in full color, Rex's main body is a dark green, and his spikes and scarf are orange. Reflect this by using darker shading on his main body and lighter shading on the orange areas. Now you're finished and ready to resume your hunt!

HOW TO DRAW:
VALKYRIE

1.

Get ready to glide into action with this cool Legendary Outfit by sketching the figure's framework.

2.

Use your framework to build your character's initial shape, with a strong hands-on-hips pose, slim waist, and strong legs.

3.

Sketch in eye and mouth placement, looking down at the viewer. Add a rough batwing shape for Valkyrie's Back Bling.

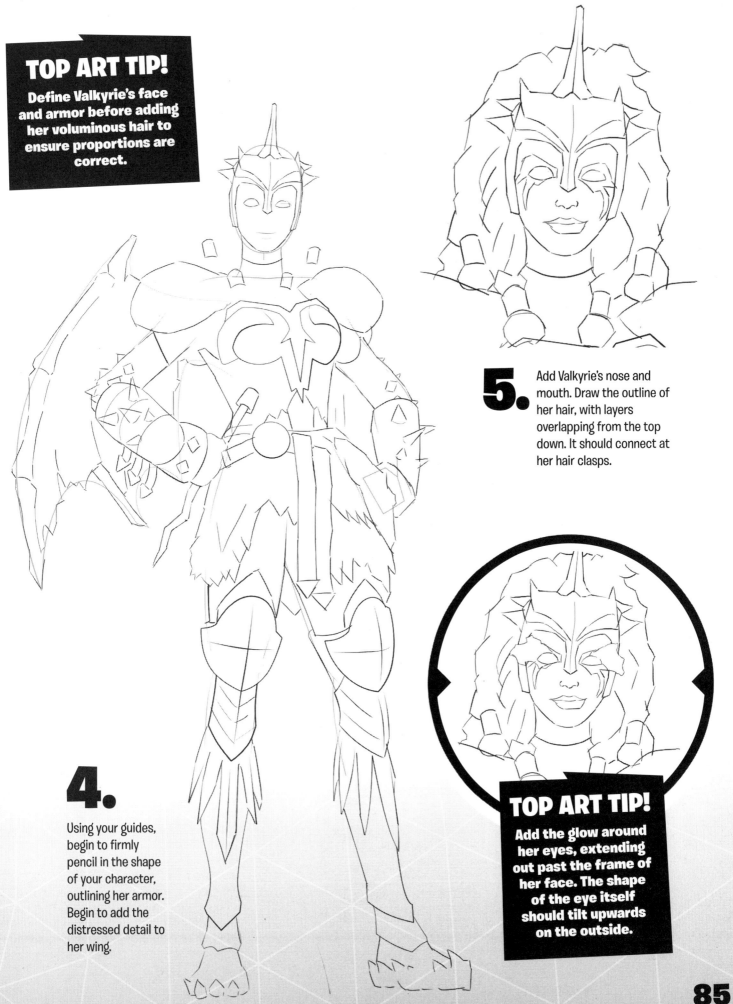

TOP ART TIP!

Define Valkyrie's face and armor before adding her voluminous hair to ensure proportions are correct.

5. Add Valkyrie's nose and mouth. Draw the outline of her hair, with layers overlapping from the top down. It should connect at her hair clasps.

4.

Using your guides, begin to firmly pencil in the shape of your character, outlining her armor. Begin to add the distressed detail to her wing.

TOP ART TIP!

Add the glow around her eyes, extending out past the frame of her face. The shape of the eye itself should tilt upwards on the outside.

TOP ART TIP!

Valkyrie's forearm armor may look intimidating to draw, but can be broken into basic shapes. Picture it as a series of cones and triangles on a cylinder.

6.

When you're happy with your character's outline, erase any rough pencil marks and add the Outfit's finer details. Add texture to her hair, torn wings, and layered armor.

TOP ART TIP!

Valkyrie's intricate knee armor is made up of lots of triangles. The armor curves in to follow the slim shape of the center of her knee.

7.

Finish by adding value to your drawing. Leaving her eyes white will create the illusion that her eyes are glowing, meaning she's ready to do battle.

HOW TO DRAW: RAVEN

1.

Draw a loose framework of your character. As a brooding master of the dark skies, his pose is menacing and inward.

2.

Build upon your initial framework and add shape to your character. Notice his wide stance and curved spine.

TOP ART TIP!

Although Raven's right leg is straight, there is still lots of definition around the knee.

3.

Begin to finalize your character's shape by penciling in a firm outline. Take care with the extended fingers here.

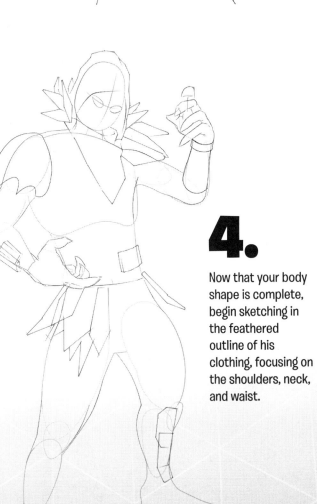

4.

Now that your body shape is complete, begin sketching in the feathered outline of his clothing, focusing on the shoulders, neck, and waist.

5.

Now start adding details, including belts and patches.

6.

When you are happy with your figure, firmly mark your overall outline and erase any rough lines. Add finer details to the Outfit.

7.

Add solid blacks to the underside of Raven's feathers and his face. Take care to lightly define the shape of his face against the inner hood by changing your pencil stroke.

8.

Start adding value to the Outfit, adding a base layer of shading. Begin by lightly lining Raven's darkest areas.

9.

Add value to the rest of your Outfit and begin your final polish. Use your pencil strokes to show the rough texture of Raven's outer layer. Leave his eyes white for a startling contrast that will strike fear into the hearts of your enemies.

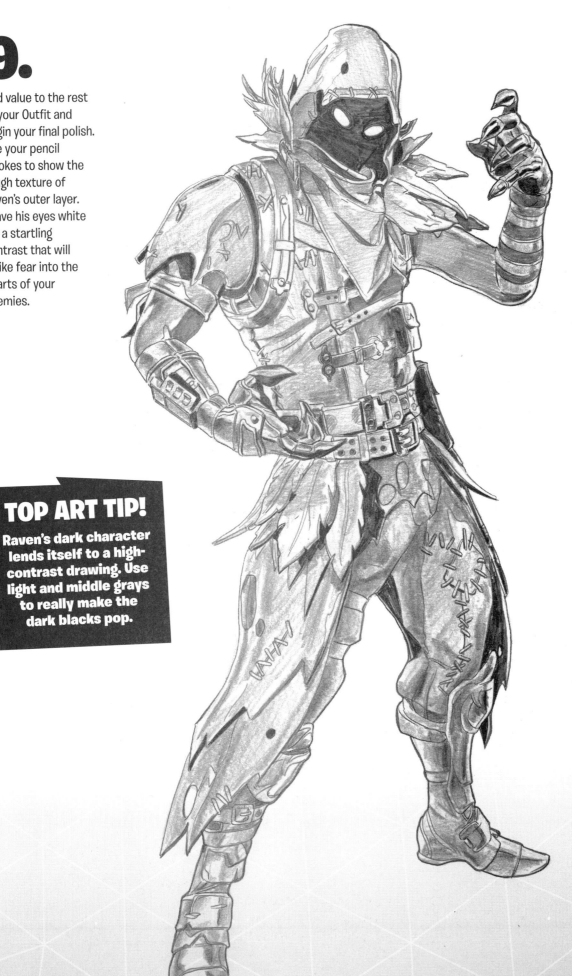

TOP ART TIP!

Raven's dark character lends itself to a high-contrast drawing. Use light and middle grays to really make the dark blacks pop.

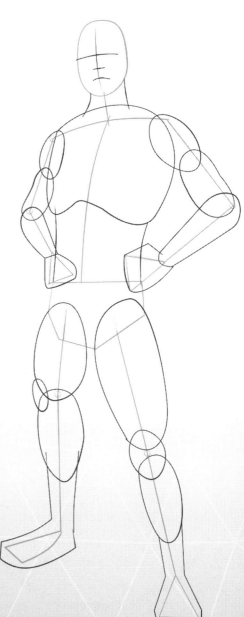

HOW TO DRAW:
SKULL TROOPER

1.

Begin your spooky Skull Trooper drawing by sketching a loose framework of your character.

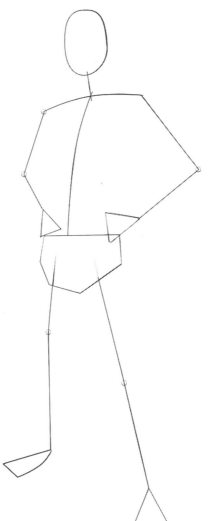

2.

Build upon your framework, adding shape to your character. It is worth defining Skull Trooper's broad shoulders, heavy chest, and muscular arms and legs at this stage.

TOP ART TIP!

Muscular character outlines usually follow the skeleton shape, curving out where the body is more muscular and tapering at the joints.

3.

Begin to finalize the outline of your character's body. His head is more skeletal than round. Begin defining this shape here.

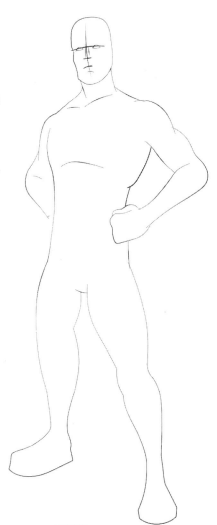

TOP ART TIP!

Both of Skull Trooper's belt buckles begin as basic square shapes. Add curves to the top and sides of the first to create an X, and simply draw a smaller square and two thin rectangles to create the second.

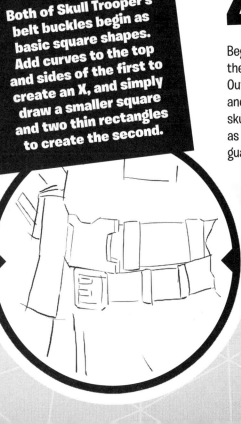

4.

Begin sketching in the outlines for your Outfit's accessories and details. Add the skullcap and a scarf, as well as large shin guards and boots.

5.

To draw Skull Trooper's cool skeleton facepaint, sketch in basic facial features and gradually build them into a skeletal face. Use a prism to draw his large, wide nose, rounding off the edges.

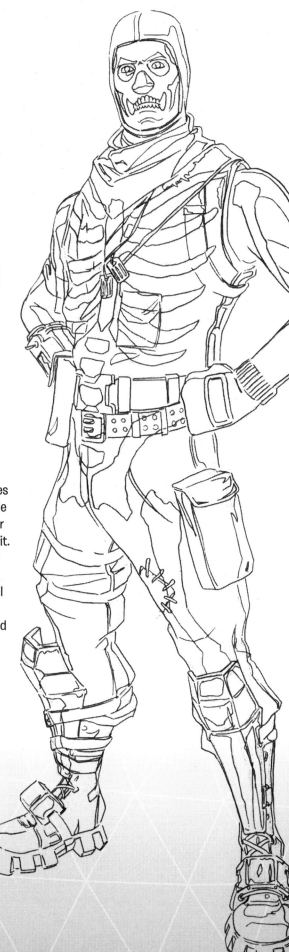

6.

Firm up your outlines and erase any visible guidelines. Add finer details to your Outfit. Skull Trooper's bold costume requires very few light pencil marks for texture, preferring bold, solid lines.

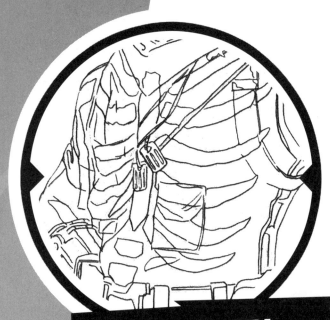

TOP ART TIP!

Make six evenly spaced marks on each side of the vertebrae in the middle of Skull Trooper's outfit. Use these as a guide for drawing your ribs, curving the lines upwards.

7.

Finish by shading the entire figure, working from the top to the bottom. For this dark Outfit, use thick blacks and hard grays for the body, and use a soft pencil to gently shade the skeleton detail painted on Skull Trooper's costume.

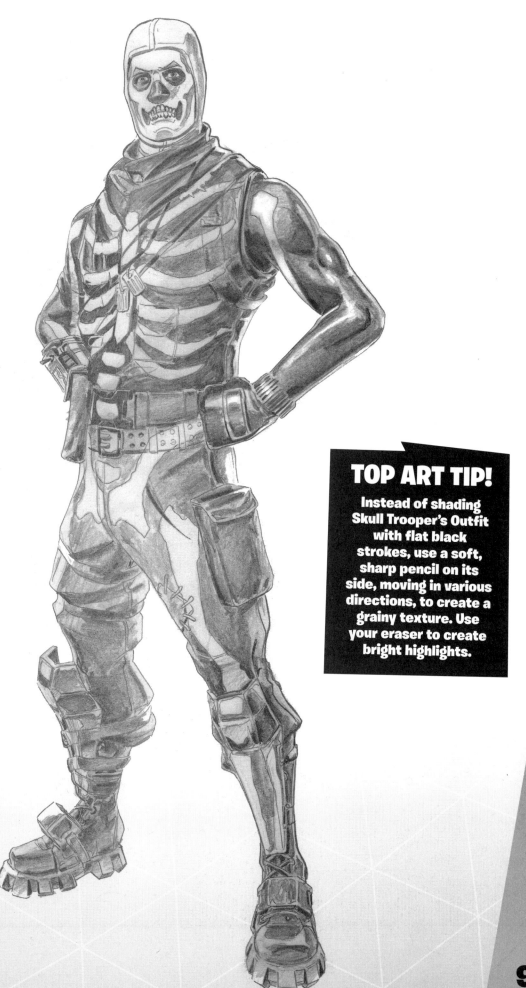

TOP ART TIP!

Instead of shading Skull Trooper's Outfit with flat black strokes, use a soft, sharp pencil on its side, moving in various directions, to create a grainy texture. Use your eraser to create bright highlights.

HOW TO DRAW:
ALL TERRAIN
KART

1.

Using a straight edge, identify your horizon line and lightly pencil in a two-point perspective grid. The kart will be below eye level.

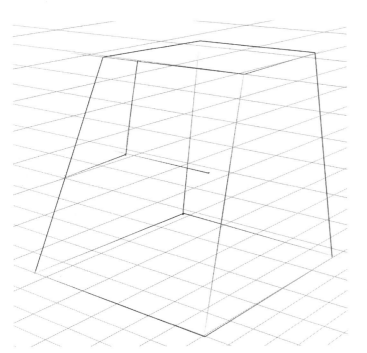

2. Using your guidelines, sketch a cube with the front face sloping out towards us. This will provide the base outline for your kart.

3. Begin to sketch the kart's basic shape, with a large square for the roof and three cylinders for the wheels. Rounded rectangles create the seat and back support.

4.

Complete the kart's outline. Use your grid to help with foreshortening when drawing diagonal lines on the kart's frame. A sphere and cylinder creates the engine shape.

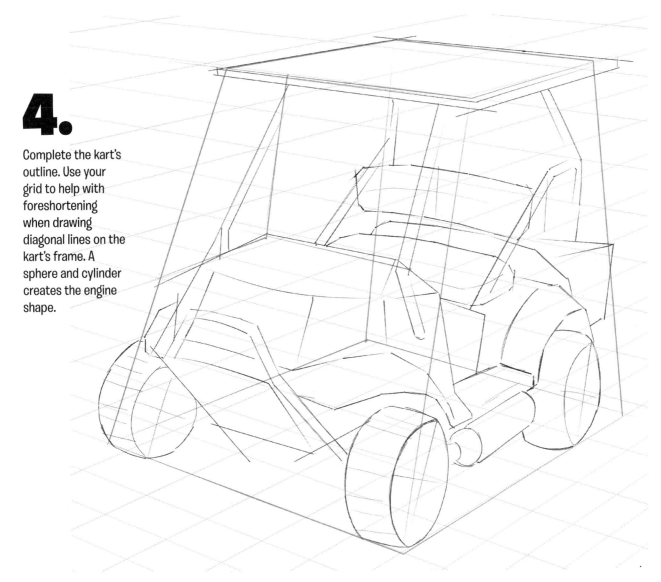

5.

Once you are happy with your overall outline, erase the grid and guidlines. Sketch in additional details, including the steering wheel, flag, and the hanging Beef Boss and Tomato Head charms.

TOP ART TIP!

Use soft angles to create the rounded appearance of the back of the kart. Cylinders and curved rectangles can help add shape.

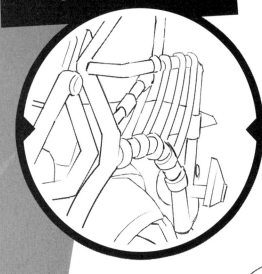

6.

Begin to finalize your kart. Building upon your outline, add shape to the seating area, as well as definition to the wheels and hood. Don't forget the llama head!

7.

Firm up your pencilwork and add finishing details. Lightly outline where dark shadows will fall on the seat before moving onto shading.

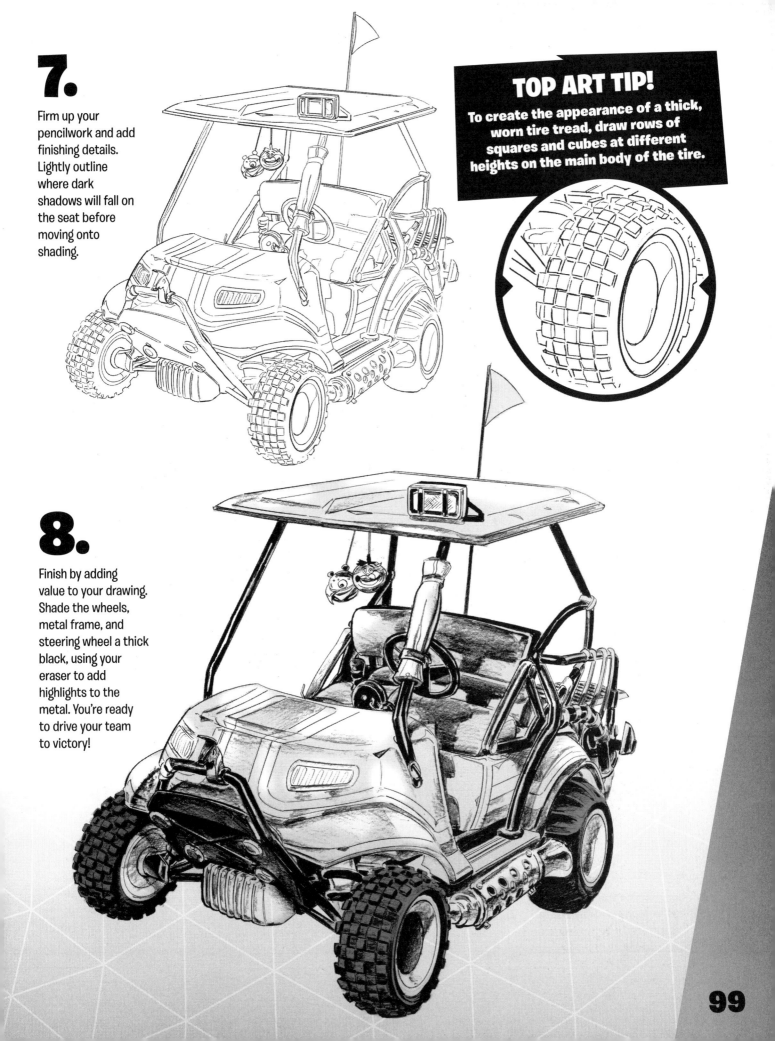

TOP ART TIP!

To create the appearance of a thick, worn tire tread, draw rows of squares and cubes at different heights on the main body of the tire.

8.

Finish by adding value to your drawing. Shade the wheels, metal frame, and steering wheel a thick black, using your eraser to add highlights to the metal. You're ready to drive your team to victory!

1.

Using a straight edge, identify your horizon line and lightly pencil in a two-point perspective grid. The vehicle will be at eye level.

2.

Draw a large cube. Notice that the lines on the far edge are slightly angled. This will provide the base outline for your vehicle.

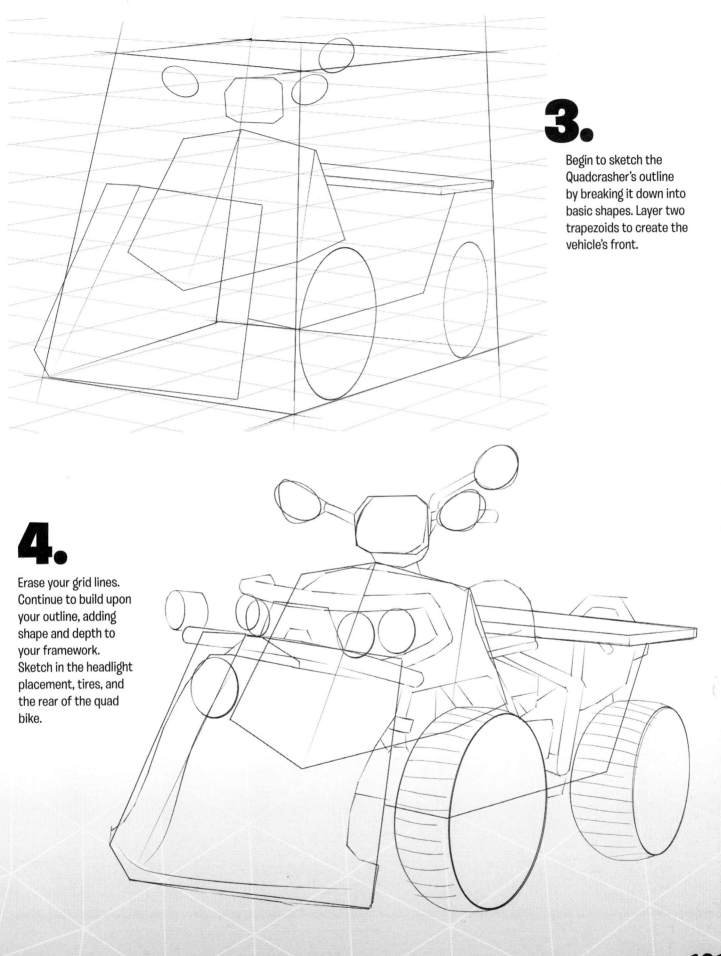

3.

Begin to sketch the Quadcrasher's outline by breaking it down into basic shapes. Layer two trapezoids to create the vehicle's front.

4.

Erase your grid lines. Continue to build upon your outline, adding shape and depth to your framework. Sketch in the headlight placement, tires, and the rear of the quad bike.

5.

Finalize the basic shape of your drawing. Erase any visible guidelines and begin adding details to your Quadcrasher.

6.

Keep refining the details. Remember that Quadcrasher is designed to smash through buildings, so don't worry if your lines aren't perfect. This can be disguised as wear and tear.

7.

Firmly pencil in the final outline and add finishing details, including the wide eyes and spiral in the center of the front wheel. Very lightly outline value areas on the quad bike's body.

8.

Add value to your Quadcrasher, working from top to bottom. Shade darkly around the eyes and mouth to create a menacing appearance.

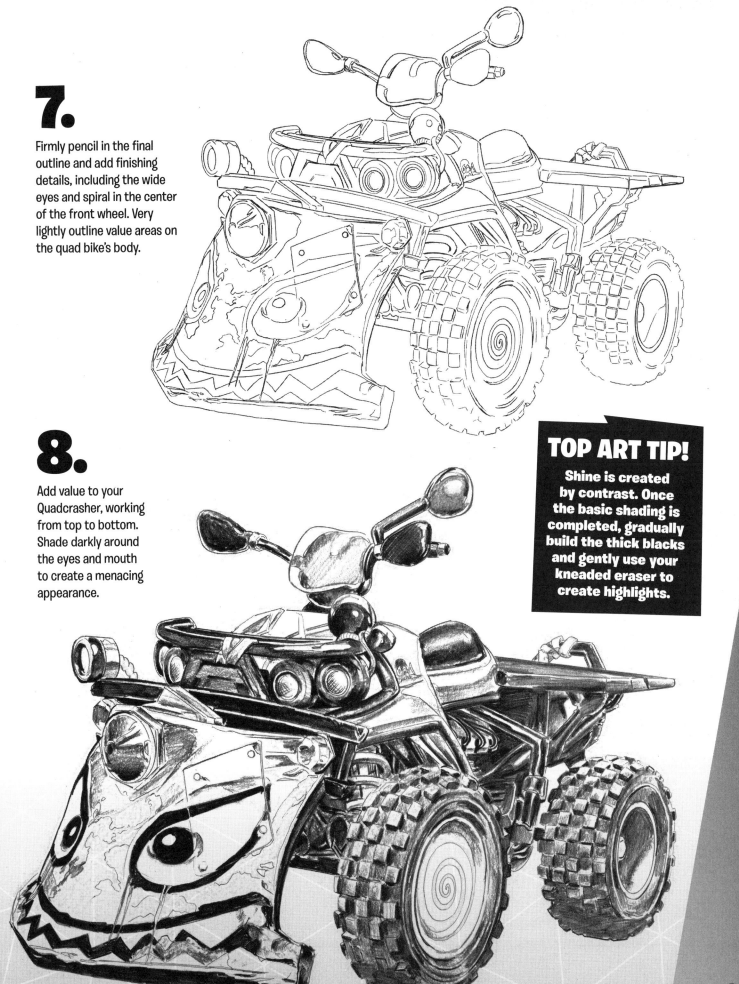

TOP ART TIP!

Shine is created by contrast. Once the basic shading is completed, gradually build the thick blacks and gently use your kneaded eraser to create highlights.

103

HOW TO DRAW:

THE BATTLE BUS

TOP ART TIP!
When everything converges towards one vanishing point, it is known as one-point perspective.

1.

Begin by drawing a one-point perspective grid. The vanishing point has been highlighted. Draw a second grid of evenly-spaced rectangles. This will help to determine the appropriate height of your bus when you come to draw the vehicle's outline.

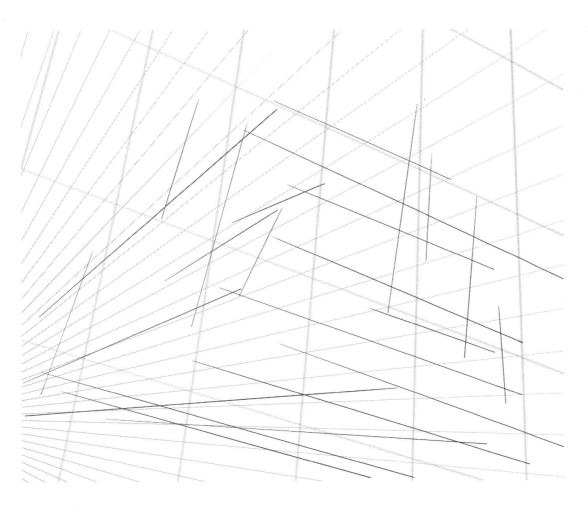

2.

Use loose light lines to roughly sketch the basic framework for the Battle Bus. Your guidelines will help you with foreshortening as the back of the bus shrinks toward the vanishing point. All these lines may look daunting, but this will soon transform into a large, floating bus.

3.

Using your guidelines, start adding real shape to your vehicle. Round off the edges of the rectangles that create the shape of the bus's body. Add four thin cylinders for wheels.

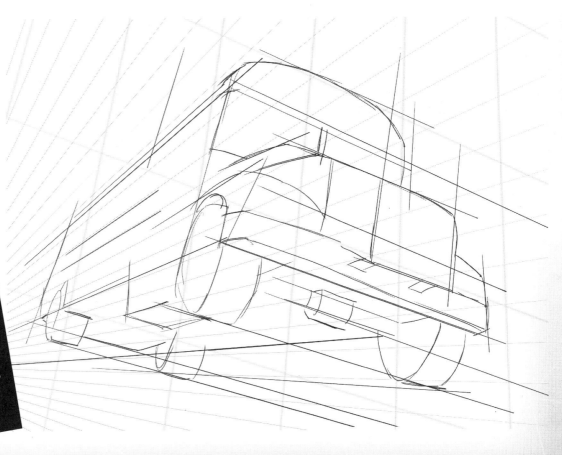

TOP ART TIP!

Your horizon line will become the left underside of the bus. Use this as your starting point and build the lines around it.

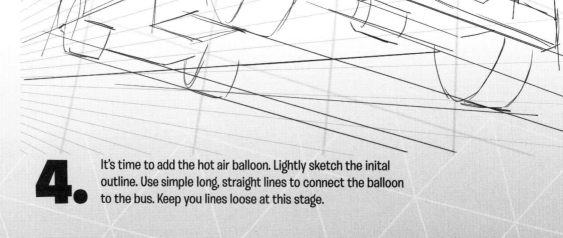

TOP ART TIP!

A large circle makes up the main body of a hot air balloon. Add a triangle at the base to create the overall balloon shape, replacing the point with a hexagon.

4. It's time to add the hot air balloon. Lightly sketch the inital outline. Use simple long, straight lines to connect the balloon to the bus. Keep you lines loose at this stage.

5.

Begin lightly sketching details onto your vehicle, including the satellite and wheel clamps. Continue to use your guidelines to roughly add a row of windows.

HOW TO DRAW:
THE
BATTLE
BUS

TOP ART TIP!
Use a straight edge, such as a ruler, for your hard lines. Using tools will help with foreshortening and make the finished product look accurate.

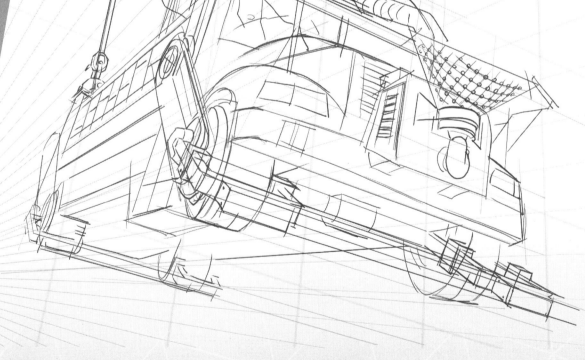

6. Your drawing should be taking shape now. Continue to build upon your intial sketches to add smaller details to your Battle Bus, such as the sections of tubing that run from the grille to the hot air balloon.

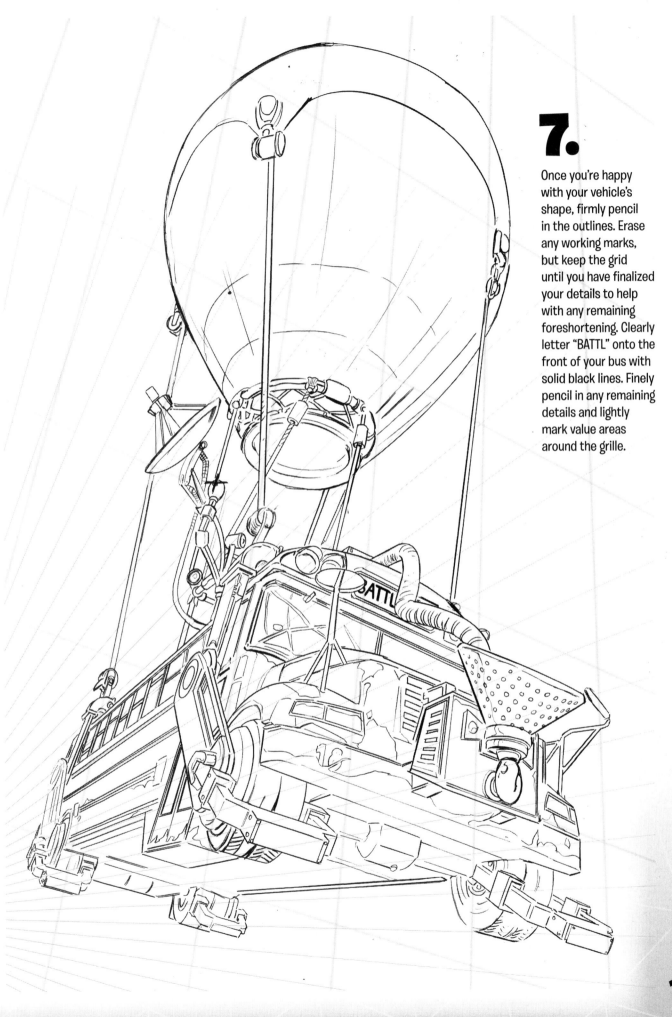

7.

Once you're happy with your vehicle's shape, firmly pencil in the outlines. Erase any working marks, but keep the grid until you have finalized your details to help with any remaining foreshortening. Clearly letter "BATTL" onto the front of your bus with solid black lines. Finely pencil in any remaining details and lightly mark value areas around the grille.

THE
BATTLE
BUS

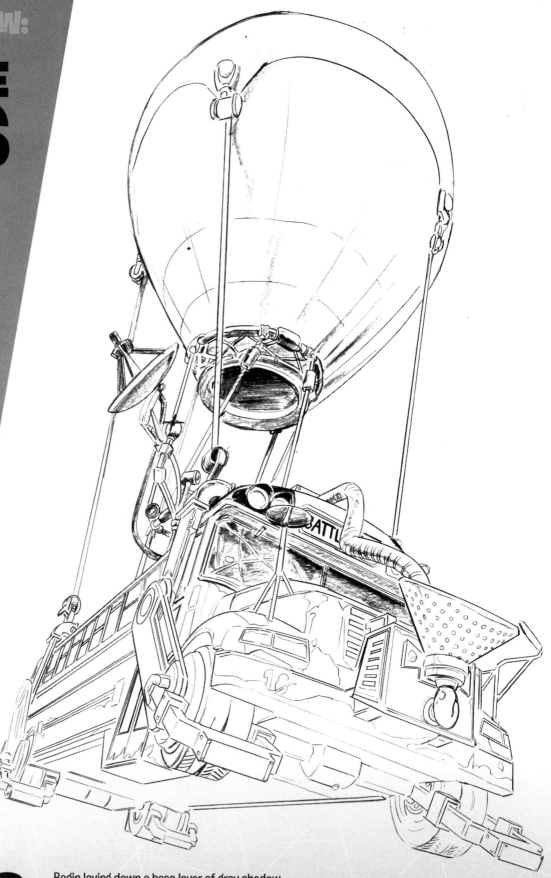

8. Begin laying down a base layer of gray shadow. To define the cracks in the windshield, shade the glass darkly and leave the areas around the cracked glass a bright white.

9.

Finish by adding value to your illustration. Curved vertical lines of gradation will help add shape to one side of the balloon. Keep the other side a crisp, bright white to reflect light.

TOP ART TIP!

Use gradual shading transitions to portray a round edge, giving it a smooth look. Abrupt shading transitions are best for conveying sharp edges.

First published in the UK in 2019 by WILDFIRE an imprint of HEADLINE PUBLISHING GROUP

Cataloguing in Publication Data is available from the British Library

Paperback 978 14722 6528 9

Written by Kirsten Murray

Illustrations by Mike Collins

Design by Amazing15

All images © Epic Games, Inc.

Printed and bound in Slovenia

HEADLINE PUBLISHING GROUP
An Hachette UK Company
Carmelite House
50 Victoria Embankment
London, EC4 0DZ
www.headline.co.uk www.hachette.co.uk

Little, Brown and Company
Hachette Book Group
1290 Avenue of the Americas, New York, NY 10104
Visit us at LBYR.com

www.epicgames.com

First Edition: July 2019

First U.S. Edition: July 2019

Little, Brown and Company is a division of Hachette Book Group, Inc.

The Little, Brown name and logo are trademarks of Hachette Book Group, Inc.

ISBN: 978-0-316-42516-2

U.S. edition printed in the United States of America

All images © Epic Games, Inc.

CW
UK: 10 9 8 7 6 5 4 3 2 1
U.S.: 10 9 8 7 6 5 4 3 2 1